FIELD HEARING ON EMPLOYMENT DISCRIMINATION IN LAW ENFORCEMENT AGENCIES

MONDAY, JUNE 13, 1994

HOUSE OF REPRESENTATIVES,
SUBCOMMITTEE ON SELECT
EDUCATION AND CIVIL RIGHTS,
COMMITTEE ON EDUCATION AND LABOR,
Brooklyn, NY.

The subcommittee met, pursuant to call, at 10:20 a.m., in Atrium-Alphi-Theater, New York City Technical College, 300 Jay Street, Brooklyn, New York, Hon. Major R. Owens, Chairman, presiding.

Members present: Representatives Owens and Payne.

Staff present: Maria Cuprill; Braden Goetz; Wanser R. Green; and Ronald Bailey.

Chairman OWENS. The hearing of the Subcommittee on Select Education and Civil Rights will come to order.

Today's hearing is focused on the subject of discrimination within law enforcement agencies.

In fighting crime, the cop on the beat is unquestionably the most important component of the entire crime-fighting effort. Improving the productivity and the performance of the cop on the beat requires more than merely new methods of training. Before the Federal Government, under the provisions presently being considered by the House and the Senate, provides 100,000 additional police personnel across the country in local law enforcement agencies, it is important that taxpayers closely examine all aspects of this vital human element of the crime-fighting efforts.

The Equal Employment Opportunity Commission can clearly assist the process of improving the personnel performance of law enforcement agencies. In the course of performing its mandated duties with respect to discrimination in agencies receiving Federal funds, the Equal Employment Opportunity Commission must be encouraged by Congress to go where it has seldom ventured before.

Discrimination in the recruitment, training, or promotional practices of the city or State police has a direct bearing on the capability of these agencies to effectively fight crime. To hire and retain more knowledgeable and sensitive personnel provides better police protection for the public.

In addition to this very practical consideration, we must also note that such discrimination is prohibited by Federal and State laws.

The law enforcement agencies, as paramilitary organizations, present a special challenge for those entities seeking to combat discrimination. This subcommittee has chosen to focus on this complex problem in order to maximize creative guidance through the congressional oversight process.

Today's hearing is the fourth in a series we have held over the past year. Although EEOC is presently a ship without a captain, we do expect a priority setting process to begin soon. We are insisting that in setting these priorities, combating discrimination in law enforcement must be a first priority. This initiative must be escalated before the Federal Government begins to fund 100,000 new police positions for local governments.

Particularly in the City of New York, the need for a new initiative has been dramatized by the exposure of widespread corruption within the police department and by the higher frequency of police brutality incidents within the last few months.

The death of Ernest Sayon is a highly visible example of police insensitivity which produced deadly consequences. In New York City, a culture of contempt for minorities and for low-income communities has generated a pattern of victimization in the police department confined primarily to minorities and poor people.

Deaths in the custody of police, for example, and police brutality allegations almost never occur in majority, white, middle-class neighborhoods. Obviously there is a problem of personnel sensitivity which may be related to the racial, religious, ethnic and sexual composition of the police force.

This hearing continues the exploration of a complex set of special circumstances operating within the closed confines of the paramilitary law enforcements organizations which limits the numbers of minorities and women who are recruited, promoted and retained.

[The prepared statement of Hon. Major R. Owens follows:]

Statement of Hon. Major R. Owens, a Representative in Congress from the State of New York

In fighting crime, the cop on the beat is unquestionably the most important component of the entire crime-fighting effort. Improving the productivity and the performance of the cop on the beat requires more than merely new methods of training. Before the Federal Government, under the provisions proposed in the anti-crime program presently under consideration, provides funding for 100,000 additional police personnel, it is important that taxpayers closely examine all aspects of this vital human element.

The Equal Employment Opportunity Commission can clearly assist this process of improving the personnel performance of law enforcement agencies. In the course of performing its mandated duties with respect to discrimination in agencies receiving Federal funds, the EEOC must be encouraged by Congress to go where it has seldom ventured before. Discrimination in the recruitment or the training or promotional practices of the city or State police has a direct bearing on the capability of these agencies to effectively fight crime. To hire and retain more knowledgeable and sensitive personnel provides better police protection for the public. In addition to this very practical consideration, we must also note that such discrimination is prohibited by Federal and State laws.

The law enforcement agencies, as paramilitary organizations, present a special challenge for those entities seeking to combat discrimination. This Subcommittee on Select Education and Civil Rights has chosen to focus on this complex problem in order to maximize creative guidance through the congressional oversight process. Today's hearing is the fourth in a series we have held over the past year. Although EEOC is presently a ship without a captain, we do expect a priority setting process to begin soon. We are insisting that combating discrimination in law enforcement must be a first priority. This initiative must be escalated before the Federal Government begins to fund 100,000 new police positions for local governments.

Particularly in New York City the need for a new initiative has been dramatized by the exposure of widespread corruption within the police department; and by the

FIELD HEARING ON EMPLOYMENT DISCRIMINATION IN LAW ENFORCEMENT AGENCIES

HEARING

BEFORE THE

SUBCOMMITTEE ON SELECT EDUCATION AND CIVIL RIGHTS

OF THE

COMMITTEE ON EDUCATION AND LABOR
HOUSE OF REPRESENTATIVES

ONE HUNDRED THIRD CONGRESS

SECOND SESSION

FIELD HEARING HELD IN BROOKLYN, NEW YORK, JUNE 13, 1994

Serial No. 103–92

Printed for the use of the Committee on Education and Labor

U.S. GOVERNMENT PRINTING OFFICE

84–118 CC WASHINGTON : 1994

For sale by the U.S. Government Printing Office
Superintendent of Documents, Congressional Sales Office, Washington, DC 20402
ISBN 0-16-046114-6

COMMITTEE ON EDUCATION AND LABOR

WILLIAM D. FORD, Michigan, *Chairman*

WILLIAM (BILL) CLAY, Missouri
GEORGE MILLER, California
AUSTIN J. MURPHY, Pennsylvania
DALE E. KILDEE, Michigan
PAT WILLIAMS, Montana
MATTHEW G. MARTINEZ, California
MAJOR R. OWENS, New York
THOMAS C. SAWYER, Ohio
DONALD M. PAYNE, New Jersey
JOLENE UNSOELD, Washington
PATSY T. MINK, Hawaii
ROBERT E. ANDREWS, New Jersey
JACK REED, Rhode Island
TIM ROEMER, Indiana
ELIOT L. ENGEL, New York
XAVIER BECERRA, California
ROBERT C. SCOTT, Virginia
GENE GREEN, Texas
LYNN C. WOOLSEY, California
CARLOS A. ROMERO-BARCELÓ, Puerto Rico
RON KLINK, Pennsylvania
KARAN ENGLISH, Arizona
TED STRICKLAND, Ohio
RON DE LUGO, Virgin Islands
ENI F. H. FALEOMAVAEGA, American Samoa
SCOTTY BAESLER, Kentucky
ROBERT A. UNDERWOOD, Guam

WILLIAM F. GOODLING, Pennsylvania
THOMAS E. PETRI, Wisconsin
MARGE ROUKEMA, New Jersey
STEVE GUNDERSON, Wisconsin
RICHARD K. ARMEY, Texas
HARRIS W. FAWELL, Illinois
CASS BALLENGER, North Carolina
SUSAN MOLINARI, New York
BILL BARRETT, Nebraska
JOHN A. BOEHNER, Ohio
RANDY "DUKE" CUNNINGHAM, California
PETER HOEKSTRA, Michigan
HOWARD P. "BUCK" McKEON, California
DAN MILLER, Florida
MICHAEL N. CASTLE, Delaware

PATRICIA F. RISSLER, *Staff Director*
JAY EAGEN, *Minority Staff Director*

SUBCOMMITTEE ON SELECT EDUCATION AND CIVIL RIGHTS

MAJOR R. OWENS, New York, *Chairman*

DONALD M. PAYNE, New Jersey
ROBERT C. SCOTT, Virginia
THOMAS C. SAWYER, Ohio

CASS BALLENGER, North Carolina
BILL BARRETT, Nebraska
HARRIS W. FAWELL, Illinois

CONTENTS

higher frequency of police brutality incidents within the last few months. The death of Ernest Sayon is a highly visible example of police insensitivity which produced deadly consequences. In New York City, a culture of contempt for minorities and for low-income communities has generated a pattern of victimization confined primarily to minorities and poor people. Deaths in the custody of police and police brutality allegations almost never occur in majority, white, middle-class neighborhoods. Obviously there is a problem of personnel sensitivity which may be related to the racial, religious, ethnic and sex composition of the police force.

This hearing continues the exploration of a complex set of special circumstances operating within the closed confines of the paramilitary law enforcement organizations which limits the number of minorities and women who are recruited, promoted and retained.

Chairman OWENS. We are pleased to welcome those witnesses who have chosen to appear today. After their confirmation, you have been given at the desk a list of witnesses. I will read the entire list of witnesses.

A hearing of this nature is limited by the fact that we can only schedule it for two or three hours. There are pressing matters that Members of the House of Representatives must attend to and we could not schedule an all-day hearing.

This is the fourth hearing on this subject. It will not be the last. We will have additional hearings.

Those witnesses who would not or could not testify, or those who did not know about the hearing, will have another opportunity if they wish. The list of witnesses that have been invited and who have consented to testify in the first panel—I will call the entire list of witnesses and then we will call for those who are here, the first group.

Before we do that, I am pleased to welcome my colleague, a member of the Subcommittee on Select Education and Civil Rights from the great State of New Jersey, Mr. Donald Payne.

If he wants to get a chance to catch his breath before an opening statement, we will let him do that or he can make his opening statement now.

Congressman Payne.

Mr. PAYNE. Thank you very much, Mr. Chairman. Thank you for calling this very important hearing.

I apologize for being a little bit late. This is the third hearing that we have had surrounding the oversight of the EEOC and employment discrimination in law enforcement and I am honored and proud to be a part of this very important process.

I would like to extend a warm welcome to Mr. Alvin Smith, a New Jersey State Trooper from my district. Mr. Smith, I would like to thank you for your participation in this whole process. I know that you have been down to Washington a few times to testify and we appreciate what you and your fellow troopers are doing to try to see that justice prevails.

The EEOC truly plays an important role in this country and was created to protect the civil rights of employees. Sometimes the only avenues for individuals experiencing discrimination in the workplace who are unable to afford an attorney is to take their complaint to these Federal agencies to have their claims investigated.

The past subcommittee hearings, notably in July 1993 and March 1994, have revealed some blatant and outrageous forms of discrimination and humiliation to African-American and other minority individuals.

Throughout these hearings, I have witnessed true abilities of courage. It takes a brave person to bring a civil rights claim against their employer. The individual fears retribution, termination or the tarnishing of their career.

According to past accounts already told to the subcommittee by some of the New Jersey State Troopers, some have already been faced with serious retribution. I really hope that these hearings will help us develop methods and procedures for improving the EEOC investigation process and discovering ways to increase its effectiveness.

Additionally, the various testimony from individuals that have experience with the EEOC process, as well as having pending claims with the agency, have been invaluable for members of this subcommittee. Thus far, these witnesses have provided a real personal element for civil rights enforcement which sometimes gets lost in the maze of litigation.

I would like to thank the witnesses for their participation and would like to commend the Chairman again. I look forward to the proceedings of this hearing.

Chairman OWENS. Thank you very much, Congressman Payne.

As Congressman Payne noted, we have had previous hearings. One of the first hearings involved New Jersey State Troopers who have experienced reprisals. One of the reasons that we did not single out individuals and publicly invite them was because we did not want to put them on the spot.

There were a number of people who were invited because they heard about previous hearings and asked to testify in future hearings. We invited others because they were recommended as people who were knowledgeable.

There were a number of people invited specifically because they are former police officers or former members of law enforcement organizations with nothing to fear, no reason to worry about reprisals.

I will read the list of people who were extended invitations and said they would be here.

Commissioner William Bratton's office said that he would be here but contacted us on Friday saying he would send a representative. Is there a representative from the New York City Police Department here? There is no representative here at this time.

Sergeant Grace Ridley, President, Guardians Association, New York City Police Department. Please be seated.

Officer Wanda Burgos of the Hispanic Society previously notified us that she would testify, but notified us this morning that she would not be able to testify.

Captain Dianne Kevelier, President, Guardians Association, New York City Corrections Department is not here, but she has a representative to testify.

Is Levora Lilly-Elmore, the Recording Secretary of the Guardians Association, ready to testify?

We also note that Mr. Alvin Smith, former New Jersey State Trooper is here. Mr. Smith, will you be seated.

Mr. SMITH. Present.

Chairman OWENS. Brave enough to be here.

With Mr. Surgeon is Paula White-Ruiz——

Mr. SURGEON. Yes.

I have a former police officer, Diane Boddie, and another police officer, Officer Tyler, who would like to testify.

Chairman OWENS. This will be our first panel.

The second panel will include Osvaldo Rodriguez; Officer Eric Sanders, New York City Police Department; and Officer Paula White-Ruiz, the New York City Police Department.

That concludes the list. We will begin with the people who are here on the first panel.

Mr. Alvin Smith, would you begin please. Each member has been invited to submit testimony in writing. In some cases, they were unable to do that. We will accept your testimony in writing in the next 10 days, if you are able to submit it in the next 10 days. You may proceed without it.

If you have your testimony in writing, it will be entered into the record in its entirety. You can take the time to highlight the statement or make other comments.

Mr. Alvin Smith, New Jersey State Trooper.

STATEMENT OF ALVIN SMITH, FORMER NEW JERSEY STATE TROOPER

Mr. SMITH. Honorable Chairman Owens, Congressman Payne, and members of the subcommittee, we appreciate the opportunity to once again come before you to address the issues of discriminatory practices within the New Jersey State Police and to respond to previous testimony submitted to this subcommittee by the State police.

I would like to acknowledge other troopers here today in the audience: Glen Johnson, Darrell Beard, Mike Travis, Sammy Davis, Greg Sanders, and Arnie Abram. My attorney, Rene Steinhagen, and our Commandant, Charles Webster, is also here.

First we would like to discuss some of the misleading statistics in reference to the number of African-American men and women that have been hired within recent years which prompted the State Police to ask the U.S. District Court to lift a consent decree that had ordered increases in minority representation from within the division.

The State police have given previous testimony to the subcommittee about the minority composition of the State police which had increased to 14.6 percent since 1990. The State police would have you believe that this was accomplished through some sort of aggressive recruitment program.

Let's look at the facts. There was a four-year lapse between the 112th State police class that graduated from the academy in February of 1989, and the 113th class that graduated in January 1993.

During this time period, there were numerous retirements and dismissals. This attrition is the only factor that contributed to the rising percentage of so-called minorities. Not one trooper was hired during this time period. What then, can the State police take credit for? The answer: manipulation of statistics.

The State police have stated they are proud of their ability to promote so-called qualified minorities. One must first ask, what is a qualified minority? There certainly is no set criteria to become eligible for promotion within the State police in New Jersey.

No one has ever seen a written objective criteria on what one should or should not do throughout his career to become qualified for promotion.

What then is the criteria to become qualified? It certainly can't be discipline. We have seen numerous troopers that have documented histories of disciplinary problems; yet, they have been promoted time and time again. Of course, none of these persons are African-Americans.

Otherwise, how can the State police explain a white lieutenant who was promoted from the rank of Trooper II to Sergeant with nine years of service, compared to the 12-year average, and then promoted to the rank of lieutenant within a four-year period.

In fact, statistics presented by the State police to the subcommittee on a previous occasion indicated that there were 300 or so people that were promoted and of those promotions, 10 percent were African-American or what they call minorities, coming out to approximately 38 promotions.

However, what they don't tell you is that they are counting the actual promotions and not the individual people promoted. They promoted some people multiple times, in some cases two or three times; they were counting each one as a promotion. However, this was the same person promoted over and over again.

The fact is that there is no objective criteria that ensures fair assignment to specialist positions or promotion to higher ranks.

We would further emphasize that this is not a minority problem necessarily. This problem affects the entire division of the State police.

The State police would rather spend countless man-hours devising and revising convoluted and contorted statistics in an attempt to justify this one incontrovertible fact: The superintendent has the power to hire, fire, promote, demote, reassign, and transfer at will.

The State police promotes whomever they want whenever they want and wherever they want. That is why many of their employees have and will fall victim to racism, sexism, nepotism, cronyism and any other "ism" you can think of which under the circumstances have a disparaging impact on African-American troopers.

From January 1990 to January 1994, only 18 African-Americans were promoted to the rank of sergeant or higher. Of the 18, eight of those were given promotions after an EEOC complaint was filed by us, which was in April 1993.

To date and with only one exception, there are no African-American administrative positions at any State police station or troop headquarters within the entire State of New Jersey nor has there been since 1921.

The one exception is someone who was promoted and made to drive over 125 miles each way from his home in Cape May County to his office in Essex County.

There are no African-American polygraph operators, arson investigators, major crimes investigators, composite sketch artists, fatal accident investigators, ballistic and firearms investigators, nor many other positions too numerous to name. The State police are good at manipulating statistics, but these are the facts.

Secondly, we would like to address the issue of retaliation. In a March 24, 1994 issue of the Newark State Ledger, then Major Carl Williams is quoted as stating that nobody has been retaliated against, and that he is confident that the "inflammatory" charges stated in our EEOC complaint would be found baseless.

One member was suspended indefinitely without pay and for no stated reason, just one day after testifying before this subcommittee. Charges were not preferred against him until seven months later and only after the member filed for a preliminary injunction. This member remains suspended without pay to this day.

Another member has been placed into hyper-scrutiny, disciplined for the most minor of offenses, and has been given bad performance evaluations over and over again. This member was the first African-American ever assigned to his particular specialist unit.

After filing a grievance with the Affirmative Action Office—he was first disciplined for actually complaining to the Affirmative Action Officer, for physically going to the Affirmative Action Officer to complain—he was transferred to a station 70 miles away from his house.

It was after the Affirmative Action Office then realized that he was transferred that they admitted that there was a problem with that and they rescinded the transfer.

Another member has been transferred to a station 60 miles from his home after complaining about the conduct of a lieutenant who used disparaging and degrading remarks towards him.

These "nobodies" know that they have been retaliated against. There is more, but my time is limited.

In conclusion, I would like to bring to your attention some statements made by the current Governor of New Jersey Christie Todd Whitman prior to her election.

The Monday October 4, 1993 issue of the Newark Star Ledger quotes then candidate Whitman as stating that she was "disturbed that Governor Florio has taken no action on the charges of discrimination leveled by African-American State troopers."

She further states, "I will not take you," meaning African-Americans, "for granted as Jim Florio has."

On May 3, 1994, the 115th State police class began training at the State Police Training Center in Sea Girt, New Jersey, a class that was given the okay by the Whitman administration.

Out of a total of 158 recruits, only three are African-Americans. Right now, in 1994, only three African-Americans in the State police class.

I guess all the African-American troopers are very glad that the 1975 consent decree was lifted. Now we can go back to the good old days prior to 1975 when blacks were persona non grata in the State police.

In fact, why don't we just go all the way back to when blacks were not even allowed in the State police? After all, in the words of the former Superintendent of State Police, Justin Dintino, when he was referring to the promotional system, "It has been this way since 1921." Why should we change it?

We would like to thank the committee for their time and hospitality and inviting us to testify here today about a topic very dear to all of us.

Thank you.

[The prepared statement of Mr. Smith follows:]

Alvin Smith

Honorable Chairman Owens, Congressman Payne, members of the Subcommittee: We appreciate the opportunity to once again come before you to address the issues of discriminatory practices within the New Jersey State Police, and to respond to previous testimony submitted to this sub-committee by the hierarchy of the of the State Police.

First we would like to discuss some misleading statistics in reference to the number African-American men and woman hired within recent years which prompted the State Police to ask the U.S. District Court to lift a consent decree that had ordered increases in minority representation from within the division. The State Police have given testimony that the so called minority composition of the State Police has increased to over 14.6% since 1990. The hierarchy of the State Police would have you believe that this was accomplished through some sort of aggressive recruitment program. Lets look at the facts:

There was a four (4) year lapse between the 112th State Police class that graduated the academy in February of 1989, and the 113th class that graduated in January of 1993. During this time period, there were numerous amounts of retirements, and dismissals. This attrition is the **only** factor that contributed to the rising percentage of so called minorities. **NOT ONE TROOPER WAS HIRED DURING THIS TIME PERIOD.** What then, can the State Police take credit for? The answer: Manipulation of statistics.

The State Police have stated that they are proud of their ability to promote so called "qualified minorities". One must first ask, what is a qualified minority? There certainly is no set criteria to become eligible for promotion. Has anyone ever seen a written objective criteria on what one should or should not do through out his career to become "qualified" for promotion? No. What then is the criteria to become qualified? It certainly can't be discipline. We have seen numerous Troopers that have documented histories of disciplinary problems, yet they have been promoted time and again. Of course, none of these people are African American. It certainly can't be the amount of time on the job. Otherwise how can the State Police explain a Lieutenant who was promoted from the rank of Trooper II to

Sergeant with only 9 years of service (compared to the 12 year average) and then was promoted two more ranks up to the rank of lieutenant all within a 4 year period, one of the fastest movements through the ranks in State Police history.

The fact is that there is no objective criteria, that ensures fair assignment to specialist positions, or promotion to higher ranks. We would further emphasize that this is not just a so called minority problem, this is a problem that effects the entire division of State Police. The State Police would rather spend countless man hours devising and revising convoluted and contorted statistics in an attempt to justify this one incontrovertible fact: The Superintendent has the power to hire, fire, promote, demote, reassign, and transfer at will. The State Police promotes whomever they want whenever and where ever they want. This is why many their employees have and will fall victim to racism, sexism, nepotism, cronyism and any other "ism" you can think of. From January 1990 to January 1994 only 18 African-Americans were promoted to the rank of Sergeant or higher. Of the 18, Eight (8) were given promotions **AFTER** the EEOC complaint was signed in April of 1993. To date and with only one exception, there are no African Americans in any administrative positions at any State Police station or Troop Headquarters, nor has there been since the year 1921. The one exception was made to drive over 125 miles each way from his home in Cape May County to his office in Essex County every day. There are no African-American: Polygraph operators, arson investigators, crime scene investigators, breathalyzer technicians, major crime investigators, composite sketch artists, Fatal accident investigators, Ballistic and Firearms investigators, nor many other positions too numerous to name. The State Police are good at manipulating statistics, but facts are facts.

Secondly, we would like to address the issue of retaliation. In the March 24, 1994 issue of the Newark Star Ledger, Major Carl Williams insists that **nobody** has been retaliated against, and that he is confident that the "inflammatory" charges stated in our EEOC complaint will be found baseless. No retaliation?:

- One member suspended indefinitely, without pay and for no stated reason, just one day after testifying before this subcommittee. Charges were not preferred until seven months later, and only after the member filed for a preliminary injunction. This member remains suspended without pay to this day.

- Another member had watermelon thrown into his work locker only days after testifying before this subcommittee. No one has been punished for this blatant act of racism.
- Another member has been placed under hyper-scrutiny, disciplined for even the most minor of offenses, and been given bad performance evaluations. This member was the first African American ever assigned to his specialist unit. After filing a grievance and complaining to the Affirmative Action Office; he was immediately transferred off of the unit to a station seventy (70) miles from his home.
- Another member transferred to a station sixty (60) miles from his home after complaining about the conduct of a Lieutenant who used disparaging and degrading remarks towards him.

These "Nobodies" know that they have been retaliated against. There are more, but time is limited.

In conclusion, we would like to bring attention to some of the statements made by Governor Christie Todd Whitman prior to her election. The Monday October 4th, 1993 issue of the Newark Star Ledger quotes the then Candidate Whitman as stating that she was "disturbed that Governor Florio has taken no action on the charges of discrimination leveled by African-American State Troopers". She further states, "I will not take you (African-Americans) for granted as Jim Florio has".

On May 3, 1994 the 115th State Police class began training at the State Police Training Center in Sea Girt, N.J. A class that was given the O.K. by the Whitman administration. Out of the total 158 recruits **only three (3) of them are African-American.** I guess all of the African American Troopers are glad that the 1975 Consent Decree was lifted. Now we can go back to the good old days prior to 1975 when Blacks were *persona non grata* . In fact. why don't we go all the way back to when Blacks were not even allowed into the State

Police. After all, in the words of former Superintendent Justin Dintino, Its been this way since 1921 why should we change it?

We would like to thank the Committee for their time and hospitality, and for inviting us to testify hear today about a topic that is very dear to all of us. Thank you.

Chairman OWENS. Thank you.

Ms. Levora Lilly-Elmore, you are with the Correction Guardians Association. You are taking Captain Dianne Kevelier's place?

Ms. LILLY-ELMORE. Yes.

STATEMENT OF LEVORA LILLY-ELMORE, GUARDS ASSOCIATION, NEW YORK CITY CORRECTIONS DEPARTMENT

Thank you. Good day, ladies and gentlemen. My name is Levora Lilly-Elmore, and I am in the absence of our president, Dianne Kevelier, representing the Correction Guardians Association, a fraternal organization of African-American employees in the New York City Department of Corrections where I have been employed the past 15 years in the rank of correction officer.

To Congressman Major Owens and members of the subcommittee, I wish to thank you for the opportunity to appear here today as this forum provides our organization with the unique occasion to air some of our concerns in an organized and disciplined manner.

In addressing the issue of discrimination in the law enforcement arena, I will first share with you some of the more horrific acts committed by whites against African-Americans in the New York City Department of Correction with little or no discipline meted out to the offenders.

Next I will present a statistical analysis to illustrate how discrimination impacts on the promotion process. The ills of New York City tend to prevail within the New York City Department of Correction.

As we move towards the 21st century, some 131 years since the abolishment of slavery, indeed we find that the more things change, the more they remain the same.

Allow me to acquaint you with some of the shameful activities of the city within a city.

Horrific Act No. 1: A white supervisor fashioned a noose around the necks of six inmates of color, attached the end of the rope to his body, then stated to the inmates, "If I fall, you die."

You may wonder why the Correction Guardians Association felt the need to champion the cause of those inmates. The answer is simply that we believed no response from us would have been tantamount to sending a message that such actions are okay, leaving other African-American employees open to similar abuse.

An African-American correction officer was present during this tirade. She refused to take part in the supervisor's tyranny and became the object of the supervisor's and his cronies' wrath. This matter festered many months until intense pressure from the organization led to the supervisor being placed on a year's probation, loss of 30 days vacation, the equivalent of a year's vacation allotment, and a transfer to another facility—a mere slap on the wrist.

Horrific Act No. 2: A young African-American probationary officer suffered severe trauma at the hands of a tenured white officer whose idea of a joke was to play Russian roulette with the person's life. The white officer placed a gun to the head of the probationer and pulled the trigger. Thank God, either the weapon misfired or there were no bullets in the weapon to begin with. Needless to say, the young probation officer was devastated, but he managed to compose himself long enough to report the incident to his supervisor.

The supervisor persuaded him not to pursue the issue, less he failed probation, and had him transferred out of the facility.

Horrific Act Number 3: A white officer discharged his firearm while assigned to a perimeter post, allegedly under the influence of alcohol. The officer was not sent for drug testing. Instead he was taken to a hospital trauma unit and allowed to report sick indefinitely.

African-American officers are sent for random drug testing and onsite drug testing at the slightest aberration of the rules. The option is the supervisor's.

Horrific Act No. 4: A group of anti-black persons wear tatoos of a black baby with a noose around its neck emblazoned above their forearms. Although we know people can do whatever they want to their bodies, we find it strange these persons would want an emblem on their body to remind then of the very people they so hate.

There is more. Horrific Act No. 5: A facility's water fountain in 1992 was marked, "for whites only" in the New York City Department of Corrections. The matter was corrected immediately.

Horrific Act No. 6: A white supervisor referred to a black secretary as "just another black cunt." His promotion from the rank of captain to assistant deputy warden was upheld briefly due to the courageousness of one African-American man who witnessed the incident and reported in writing what he had heard and seen. The offender is now a deputy warden awaiting promotion to warden.

Horrific Act No. 7: A white officer exposed himself to several black female officers. An investigation showed he had a history of sexual deviant behavior. After several months, he was allowed to resign with a stipulation that he cannot hold another law enforcement job. Whoopee!

Many of our people have been terminated for far less. All of these acts were reported to the organization by our membership. Some of these cases were never pursued by the member for fear of reprisal.

The following statistics are intended to show how discrimination in the Department of Correction impacts negatively as it relates to African-Americans in the promotional process. The Department of Correction is comprised of 13,108 employees. There are 10,922 uniformed employees and 2,186 civilian employees. In the uniformed ranks, there are 6,346 African-Americans, 2,522 whites, and 1,899 Hispanics. The remaining 2 percent are classified as Asians, American Indians and others.

African-Americans comprise 60 percent of the department's work force compared to 20 percent white and 18 percent Hispanic. The remaining 2 percent, as I said before, is made up of Asians, American Indians and others.

The ranks of captain and assistant deputy warden are obtained through competitive examination. I will, therefore, concentrate on the appointed ranks at the managerial level.

Of 56 deputy wardens, 33 are white, or 60 percent; 19 are African-American, or 19 percent; and 3 are Hispanic.

There are 24 wardens: 17 are white, 65 percent; 5 are African-American, 28 percent; and one is Hispanic, 7 percent.

Of four division chiefs, two are white, one is Hispanic and one African-American was recently promoted from that rank to chief of department, leaving a vacancy in the rank of division chief. There is one line for assistant deputy chief and that is held by an African-American.

There is one assistant chief and he is white. There are three deputy chiefs, two African-American, one male and one female, and one white.

In the civilian ranks there is one African-American deputy commissioner out of five. There are three African-American assistant deputy commissioners out of eight. There are six African-American directors, including acting directors, out of twenty-nine.

Given these statistics compiled April 29, 1994, it does not appear that the Department of Correction is abiding by the mandates of its Affirmative Employment Plan, which is governed by local, State and Federal law. Certainly, African-Americans are not adequately represented in policymaking positions and there does not appear to be any movement towards that end.

It should be noted as well that during the last promotion several months ago, out of nine promotees, six were white, two Hispanic and one was African-American.

Another major problem African-Americans are faced within the department is that the Equal Employment Opportunity Unit within the agency has staffing that does not reflect the majority of personnel. Many members do not feel comfortable filing complaints within the agency because the assigned investigators for the most part are persons of the same ethnicity as those who have offended them.

Of the six assigned investigators, one is of African ancestry. There has not been a permanent EEO officer for several months. The backlog of cases is indicative of the need for permanency at the top.

In February of this year, when inquiries were made about the movement of EEO complaints submitted by Correction Guardians Association members, the organization was advised that it was not uncommon for EEO complaints to be backlogged for several years, three to four years to be exact.

That does nothing towards fostering better working conditions when EEO complaints can go without resolution for several years.

The organization is in receipt of an Affirmative Employment Plan which contains policy statements of both the former mayor and former correction commissioner dated August 21, 1991 and May 13, 1992, respectively. If the department complied with the policy set forth in the AEP, there would be no need for me to be here today. Thus, it is our position that the Affirmative Employment Plan can be a viable tool to aid and combat discrimination at every level if it is enforced with sincerity.

We need the help of this subcommittee in getting the message across that discrimination will not be tolerated in the workplace. As it stands now, the descendants of the very people who fought, bled, cried and died to insure that an affirmative action policy was enacted are the people who are not receiving their fair share of the correction pie. We desperately seek your assistance.

Thank you.

Chairman OWENS. Ms. Lilly-Elmore, I have a copy of the written testimony. Does it include all the statistics that you just presented in your oral testimony?

Ms. LILLY-ELMORE. Yes.

Chairman OWENS. Thank you very much.

[The prepared statement of Ms. Lilly-Elmore follows:]

CONGRESSIONAL SUBCOMMITTEE HEARINGS

Discrimination In Law Enforcement

June 13, 1994

Testimony of the Correction Guardians Assoc.

Good Day Ladies and Gentlemen!

My name is Levora Lilly-Elmore; and I am representing the Correction Guardians Association - a fraternal organization of African-American employees in the New York City Department of Correction where I have been employed the past 15 years in the rank of Correction Officer.

To Congressman Major Owens and members of the subcommittee, I wish to thank you for the opportunity to appear here today, as this forum provides our organization with a unique occasion to air some of our concerns in an organized and disciplined manner.

In addressing the issue of discrimination in the law enforcement arena, I will, first, share with you some of the more horrific acts committed by whites against African-Americans in the New York City Department of Correction with little or no discipline meted out to the offenders. Next, I will present a statistical analysis to illustrate how discrimination impacts on the promotion process.

The New York City Department of Correction is a microcosm of the City of New York. Whatever are the ills of New York City tend to prevail within the New York City Department of Correction. As we move towards the 21st century, some 131 years since the abolishment of slavery, indeed we find that the more things change, the more they remain the same. Allow me to acquaint you with some of the shameful and unpardonable activities of the City within the City. Horrific Act #1 - A white supervisor fashioned a noose around the necks of six inmates of color, attached the end of the rope to his body, then stated to the inmates, "If I fall, you die". You may wonder why the Correction Guardians Association felt the need to champion the cause of those inmates. The answer is simply that we believed no response from us would have been tantamount to sending a message that such actions are okay, leaving others, specifically African-American employees open to similar abuse. Also, an African-American Correction Officer was present during this tyrade. She refused to take part in the supervisor's tyranny and became the object of the supervisor and his cronies' wrath. This matter festered many months until intense pressure from the organization led to the supervisor being placed on a year's probation, loss of 30 days vacation (the equivalent of a year's vacation allotment), and a transfer to another facility - a mere slap on the wrist.

Horrific Act #2 - A young African-American probationary officer suffered severe trauma at the hands of a tenured white officer whose idea of a joke was to play Russian Roulette with a person's life. The white officer placed a gun to the head of the probationer and pulled the trigger. Thank God, either the weapon misfired, or there were no bullets in the weapon. Needless to say, the young probationary officer was devastated, but he managed to compose himself long enough to report the incident to his supervisor. The supervisor persuaded him not to press the issue, less he failed probation, and had him transferred out of the facility.
Horrific Act #3 - A white officer discharged his firearm while assigned to a perimeter post, allegedly under the influence of alcohol. The officer was not sent for drug testing, instead he was taken to a hospital's trauma unit and allowed to report sick indefinitely. African-American officers are sent for drug testing at the slightest aberration of the rules. The option is the supervisor's.
Horrific Act #4 - A group of anti-black persons wear tattoo(s) of a black baby*emblazoned above their forearms. Although we know people can do whatever they want to their bodies, we find it strange these persons would want an emblem on their bodies that remind them of the very people they so hate. There is more!
Horrific Act #5 - A facility's water fountain is marked, "For whites only". The matter was corrected immediately.
Horrific Act #6 - A white supervisor referred to a black secretary as, "just another black cunt". His promotion from the rank of Captain to Assistant Deputy Warden was upheld briefly due to the courageousness of one African-American man who witnessed the incident and reported in writing what he had heard and seen. The offender is now a Deputy Warden awaiting promotion to Warden.
Horrific Act #7 - A white officer exposed himself to several black female officers. An investigation showed he had a history of sexual deviant behavior. After several months, he was allowed to resign with the stipulation that he cannot hold another law enforcement job. Many of our people have been terminated for far less. All of these acts were reported to the organization by our membership. Some of these cases were never pursued by the member for fear of reprisal.

The following statistics are intended to show how discrimination in the Department of Correction impacts negatively as it relates to African-Americans in the promotional process. The Department of Correction is comprised of 13,108 employees. There are 10,922 uniformed employees and 2,186 civilian employees. In the uniformed ranks, there are 6,346 African-Americans, 2,522 whites and 1,899 Hispanics. African-Americans comprise 60% of the department compared to 20% white and 18% Hispanic. The remaining 2% is made up Asians, American-Indians and others. The ranks of captain and assistant deputy warden are attained through competitive examination. I will, therefore, concentrate on the appointed ranks at the managerial level. Of 56 Deputy Wardens, 33 are white or 60%;

*with a noose around its neck

(cont.)

19 are African-American or 19%; and three are Hispanic. There are 24 Wardens; 17 are white (65%); five are African-American (28%); and one is Hispanic (7%). Of four Division Chiefs, two are white, one is Hispanic and one African-American was recently promoted from that rank to Chief of Department, leaving a vacancy in the rank of Division Chief. There is one line for Assistant Deputy Chief and that rank is held by an African-American. There is one Assistant Chief and he is white. There are three Deputy Chiefs; two are African-American and one is white.

In the civilian ranks, there is one African-American Deputy Commissioner out of five; there are three African-American Assistant Commissioners out of eight; there are six African-American Directors (including Acting Directors) out of 29. Given these statistics which were compiled April 29, 1994, it does not appear that the Department of Correction is abiding by the mandates of its Affirmative Employment Plan which is governed by local, state and federal law. Certainly, African-Americans are not adequately represented in policy-making positions, and there does not appear to be any movement towards that end. It should be noted as well that during the last promotions approximately three months ago, out of nine promotees, six were white, two Hispanic and one was African-American.

Another major problem African-Americans are faced with in the Department is that the Equal Employment Opportunity Unit within the agency has staffing that does not reflect the majority of personnel. Many members do not feel comfortable filing complaints within the agency because the assigned investigators for the most part are persons of the same ethnicity as those who have offended them. Of the six assigned investigators, one is of African ancestry. There has not been a permanent E.E.O. Officer for several months. The backlog of cases is indicative of the need for permanency at the top. In February of this year, when inquiries were made about the movement of E.E.O. complaints submitted by CGA members, the organization was advised that it was not uncommon for E.E.O. complaints to be backlogged for several years (3-4 years to be exact). That does nothing towards fostering better working conditions when EEO complaints can go without resolution for several years.

The organization is in receipt of an Affirmative Employment Plan which contains policy statements of both the former mayor and Correction Commissioner dated August 21, 1991 and May 13, 1992 respectively. If the Department complied with the policy set forth in the AEP, there would be no need for me to stand before you today. Thus, it is our position that the Affirmative Employment Plan can be a viable tool to aid in combatting discrimination at every level if it is enforced with sincerity. We need the help of this subcommittee in getting the message across that discrimination will not be tolerated in the workplace. As it stands now,

(cont.)

the descendants of the very people who fought, bled, cried and died to ensure that Affirmative Action policy was enacted, are the people who are not receiving their fair share of the Correction pie. We desparately seek your assistance.

Thank you!

Levora L. Lilly-Elmore
Executive Board Member
Correction Guardians Assoc.

/111-e

Chairman OWENS. Mr. Surgeon.

STATEMENT OF CLARENCE SURGEON, FORMER NEW YORK CITY POLICE OFFICER

Mr. SURGEON. Good morning, Members of Congress, members of the panel, ladies and gentlemen. It is an honor and pleasure to be here to testify as a former New York City Transit Department detective and police officer for 30½ years about my personal experience and how I felt when I was discriminated against within the New York City Transit Police Department.

I am Clarence Surgeon, a retired detective from the New York City Transit Police Department. I entered the department on April 4, 1955 and worked in uniform patrol for approximately 10 years. As a result of many arrests and citations, I was promoted to detective third grade in June of 1966.

Just to mention a few of my arrests in uniform which consist of armed robberies, assaults with a weapon, saving lives in fires, arrests for bribery, letters of praise from civilians, shakedowns of homosexuals by members of law enforcement agencies, criminal mischief of property amounting to thousands of dollars, stealing trains at night, I wondered why it took me 10 years to go from patrol division to the detective division.

Upon hearing that my partner, who was white, and who assisted me in the vandalism arrests, went to the detective division as a result of my arrests six or seven years before I did—and I was the arresting officer in these cases, while in uniform—I respectfully submitted a request to go into the detective division, but was denied.

I was promoted to detective third grade in June of 1966 I have been attempting to forget about the past 10 years. In June of 1972, I was promoted to detective second grade six years later, and in June 1990, 18 years later, I was promoted to detective first grade.

To the Members of Congress, the selected panel, ladies and gentlemen, I stand before you today and can honestly say that I have suffered racial discrimination within the New York City Transit Police Department detective division primarily in the area of promotion.

I have no problems or complaints against my coworkers. We understood each other and respected each other. The problems were with top bosses, who I believe were discriminatory.

From 1975 to 1980, Chief Garrily, former city council president, came to the New York City Transit Police Department. I was asked by Chief Garrily if I would be interested in handling a confidential investigation unit for him, starting a Confidential Investigation Unit with approximately 20 permanent members and up to 75 members of the department during raids, in which I was able to deal with approximately 12 other law enforcement agencies across the United States and travel on behalf of the Chief of the New York City Transit Police Department to Atlanta, Georgia; Boston, Massachusetts; and Washington, DC.

As the Commander of the Confidential Investigation Unit, I expected to get promoted from second grade to first grade, but due to the police layoffs, et cetera, there were no promotions. I was in command of third grade detectives assigned to the unit and also patrolmen.

We effected arrests in New Jersey, Marlboro, New York, investigations in New Haven, Connecticut and sent two detectives to Las Vegas, Nevada on a grand larceny case.

The Confidential Investigation Unit was a promising detail until 1980 when Chief Garrily left. The new chief was informed by supervisors, who wanted the detail but could not get it, that I was running the job.

When I met the new chief in the office and introduced myself, he commented, "Oh, you are Detective Surgeon." His body language was louder than his voice. I knew at that time that something was wrong.

A week or so later, a sergeant was assigned to the unit and in about two months, the unit was disbanded. I was transferred to the Pickpocket Unit and promotions were prevalent at this time. I thought that I would be promoted to first grade. I was passed over many times until I became disgruntled and filed a lawsuit for racial discrimination.

In the meantime, the officers that I trained were being promoted. The New York City Transit Police Guardians Association also filed a lawsuit in reference to discrimination on the job, disparity in punishment, promotions and selection to specialized units.

I filed a lawsuit against the chief of the department and the chief of detectives: Surgeon versus the New York City Transit Police Department.

During this time, I was passed over for promotion to first grade noticeably between 1980 to 1990, 10 years, in which we had three department chiefs. From 1982 to 1985, three years, we had one department chief and from 1975 to 1980, there was a job freeze in which we had one department chief.

In June of 1990, I was evaluated for promotion to first grade and promoted to first grade by the present police commissioner, William J. Bratton, upon recommendation of then Chief of Detectives Michael J. O'Connor. My lawsuit was a unique lawsuit against the New York City Transit Department and was later joined by the Transit Guardians lawsuit for all purposes in Federal District Court.

Mrs. Lillian Fennell, the State Division on Human Rights Regional Director, testified on my behalf. Chief Sandy Garrily, New York City Transit Police Department, also testified regarding my assignment as Commander of the Confidential Investigation Unit.

During his tenure, 1975-1980, there were no promotions due to a job freeze and layoffs.

Chief Garrily's testimony on my behalf was very positive. From 1980 to 1990, I experienced total discrimination by higher management by not being promoted many, many times to the extent that I became vocal and started asking questions about the criteria for getting promoted in the detective division. There were no set guidelines. There was no method in telling what was needed to get promoted.

Very few blacks and Puerto Ricans got promoted. Concern developed in the New York City Police Department and the New York City Housing Police Department regarding my lawsuit because that might have an effect on a decision for promoting detectives in the New York City Police Department and New York City Housing Police Department in which minorities are a majority in the lower grades, meaning third grade.

After I filed a lawsuit and during the hearings, I noticed that each promotion had its own criteria to fit the description of the person that they wanted to promote. My attorney, Lawrence Cummerbatch, and Mrs. Fennell also wanted to know about the policy, the procedure, the criteria, the method or reason for getting promoted from third grade to second grade and from second grade to first grade.

One of the answers was that it is up to the discretion of the chief of the department who has the final word on whether or not you got to be considered for promotion. Some of the other answers given were: "Well, we are going to look at his arrest records, at his personal attendance record. We are going to look at the job seniority. We are going to look at the unit seniority. We are going to look at the time in grade. We are going to look at the education. We are going to look at the sergeant's recommendation. We are going to look at the disciplinary charges, if any."

In all of those categories, I excelled. The arrest record, there was no problem; the sick record, there was no problem; job seniority, out of 5,000, I was number one; Unit seniority, I was number one; time in grade, number one; education, bachelors degree, masters in public administration degree; Sergeant's recommendation, good; disciplinary charges, none.

The lawyers asked, "What was Detective Surgeon's record like?" Their response: "Oh, he has a good record."

He was asked was there any competition for first grade? Yes. Why wasn't he promoted? We decided to promote detective so-and-so and so-and-so, and each promotion had a different criteria which was used to affect the candidate promotee.

Basically, I had fulfilled all of the so-called requirements for promotion. Each time I went to the court, there was a different criteria for promotion and I was always passed over.

In conclusion, I was the President of the National Black Police Association's Northeast Region of the National Black Police Association which consists of the following States: New York, New Jersey, Connecticut, Rhode Island, Maine, New Hampshire and Connecticut. During that time, we had discrimination across the United States as far as various departments being discriminated against. There seemed to be a pattern in one department; the same pattern in another department regarding racial discrimination, whether it would be in appointment within the detective division or promotions.

Once you take the sergeant's exam or lieutenant's exam or captain's exam, you would feel blacks would fair well in taking the exam, a lot of times coming out number one; but when it came to the oral exam, they would go from number one to the bottom of the list which would affect their standings on the final list.

These were some of the problems that we had. I had formed a panel consisting of various people in our community to find out why we were not being considered for promotions, why we were not being considered for candidates in the New York City Police Department, and where do we, as blacks, fall down once we take the test?

On this panel, we had about five lawyers, Dr. Gerald Horn, who is the President of the National Conference of Black Lawyers; Attorney Lawrence Cummerbatch, who was a civil rights activist; Attorney Jimmy Hargrove, New York City Police Department; Attorney Ken Kimberley, Puerto Rican Legal Defense Fund; and Attorney Laura Blackburn, the Metropolitan Transit Authority Board. Also, Senator Al Walden, Doctor Lyles, Psychologist, New York Police Department; Arlan Mead, Ph.D., President of New York State Black Psychologists; Dud Dudley, M.D.; Phyllis White, Supervisor, New York State Labor Staff Academy; Elsa Sharp, President of the Federation of Negro Civil Service Organizations; Dr. Roscoe Brown, President of One Hundred Black Men, and Reverend Lawrence Lucas. That panel lasted for more than a year.

The panel held various hearings with the candidates who were passed over on the police exams. It seems as though this was a pattern in the application, investigation section of the New York City Police Department regarding psychological, medical and character backgrounds.

We have published a book of several hundred pages, which was given to the New York City Police Department Commissioner, Van Ward. The panel concluded that yes, there is a problem within the New York City Police Department in many areas. It is too extensive to read now, but these are some things that I would like to bring out.

There was no objective criteria for pass-fail of the psychological assessment that has been established. Decisions about pass-fail are primarily a function of the examiners, the value and bias. Not even basic standardization conditions of objectivity are met.

What it means to pass-fail moreover has not been established, and the process for selection of urban police officers in a multicultural, multiethnic city as it now stands and the state of contradictions in terms of technology and understanding the human resources aspects of effective police selection and performance, validity and reliability of assessment in selection in general needs considerable scientific girding.

It goes on and on to criticize how we, as blacks, fail from the time that we take the test until the time that we get appointed.

Chairman OWENS. Mr. Surgeon, we are quite pleased to have a copy of that study. The committee will fully examine it.

Mr. SURGEON. At this time, I would like to introduce Diane Boddie, who was a member of the New York City Transit Police Department and has experienced an incident which she would like to bring forth to this panel, Congressman Owens.

Chairman OWENS. Welcome. You may proceed.

STATEMENT OF DIANE BODDIE-CARTER, FORMER MEMBER, NEW YORK CITY TRANSIT POLICE DEPARTMENT

Ms. BODDIE-CARTER. Good morning, congressmen, visitors and guests here. This morning I am not here to bring you statistics or to give you figures. What I am here for is to demonstrate the constant pattern of discrimination that is going on and the vicious cycle that is taking place.

I was appointed a transit police officer in 1981. At that time, of course, I was a young person and it was uncommon for a female to go into the Transit Police Department at that time, so I had to overcome a lot of obstacles in order to get my position. But once I was in that position, I took that position very seriously.

For the 8½ years that I was a member of the Transit Police Department, I received no civilian complaints. I received three minor departmental derelictions. I had no trial board hearings and no other, shall we say, scuttlebutt as it is mentioned.

My career up until May 30, 1986, had been taking pretty much a positive direction. On May 30, 1986, while pregnant and going to Port Authority bus terminal to pick up my sister, I was involved in an altercation with a soda vendor. This vendor was stationed outside of Port Authority bus terminal.

During that altercation, I enlisted the assistance of a Port Authority police officer. When the police officer came over to me, I told him that I believed that this vendor had a weapon beneath his cart and that I wanted him to produce it since he had threatened me with it.

The police officer asked me for identification. I explained that I had no identification since I was out on maternity leave, but that my car was parked around the corner; that I had a pocketbook there; that my fiance, another police officer from Boston, and my sister were in the car and could verify who I was.

At this time, the officer refused to take my complaint. He told me he wouldn't do it unless I could produce some identification showing that I was, in fact, a police officer. I explained to him that my charge should have been noted as if I were a regular citizen. My being a police officer had nothing to do with it.

I was telling him that I feel the man threatened me with bodily harm, struck me, and that he reached in his cart for what I believed to be a weapon.

This officer refused to entertain my complaint. At this point, I walked to my car. As I was walking to my car, I felt the back of my dress being yanked. It was the police officer who had followed me around the corner. He grabbed me from behind and spun me around. The first words out of my mouth were "Number one, I am pregnant; and number two, I am a police officer."

His response was, "I want to see some identification." I said, "My car is over there. I will go into my car to get the identification."

As I turned to walk towards my car, this police officer again snatched me from the back of my dress and said, "You are no dam cop. You are nothing but trash."

With that, he threw me to the ground and proceeded to pounce on my stomach. I am laying on the ground, face up, and screaming "Stop. Get off me. I am pregnant." At this point, being a police officer didn't matter. I simply was concerned with the life of my unborn child.

I am screaming, "I am pregnant. Get off of me." Every time I said I was pregnant, he said "Sure, you are," and proceeded to bounce on me again. The officer pulled out his nightstick and came across my head with it. When he did that, I grabbed the nightstick.

Of course, a tug ensued. All I could hear were screams from the crowd, "Pull her dress down." My dress now was up somewhere around the mid-torso area. "Get off her. Why don't you stop it?"

In the distance, I could now hear my sister, my fiancee and my friend, who had come running to the scene screaming, "She is a police officer. She is pregnant. She has health problems. Get off of her."

All of this was to no avail.

Eventually, additional units came to assist this police officer. Once they cuffed me, they sat me on the ground and I started complaining that I was in pain and wanted an ambulance. The sergeant who responded to the scene stated "You don't have pain. Stand up and walk to the car."

I told him I was unable to stand. His response to them was, "If she can't stand, drag her," and they dragged me to the patrol car. They stood me up against the patrol car and smashed my head against the top of the car as they put me in the car.

Getting into the car, I noticed my wrist had started to swell. I complained and said they needed to loosen the cuffs. The sergeant driving the vehicle said "She says it feels like it is broken. Why don't you break it?"

With that, the officer took the cuff and twisted it and fractured my wrist. Following this, I was taken to the Port Authority holding area and placed in a cell.

After I sat there and screamed and cried for two hours that I was, in fact, a police officer and that I wanted medical attention, they decided maybe they should call an ambulance. Again, this was not until my sister, fiancee and officer friend had responded to the Port Authority holding area and verified who I was.

Once an ambulance responded, after a lot of argument from the police officers who did not want them to take me for medical attention, I was finally taken to the hospital. At the hospital, this hostile treatment did not stop.

I wound up being admitted into the trauma unit that night. During that time, I was confined to bed rest because I had started to bleed vaginally. They had four male officers guarding me 24 hours a day. When I attempted to use the bedpan, the curtains were open and I was told that I had to use the bedpan in front of the four officers.

When I used tissues to wipe myself after using the bedpan, the officers came in the room and removed the tissues which had blood specimens on them, since the nurses had to see them to determine the amount of bleeding. They denied me visitation, telephone rights, all the basic privileges that I should have been afforded.

I was discharged from the hospital, but on that same night, I was also suspended as a transit police officer without pay. I remained suspended from May 30, 1986, until September 8 of 1986.

During this time, I remained home on bed rest and finally progressed from bed rest to the use of a wheelchair if I had to go out. On September 5, 1986, the New York District Attorney's Office dropped all charges against me, those charges being assault upon a police officer, disorderly conduct, and resisting arrest. All charges were dropped and the case was sealed. On September 5, the department reinstated me.

The New York City Transit Police Department has a rule that departmental charges must be filed within 30 days. This was the first of the inconsistencies with me. Departmental charges were not filed against me until almost two months after the incident occurred, yet the department allowed these charges to go through.

Once the charges had been dropped by the District Attorney's Office and I had been reinstated as a police officer, I was still out sick because as a result of the severe trauma that I had received during that beating, I bled vaginally every day from May 30, 1986 to November 13, 1986, when I gave birth to that child.

When I gave birth to the child, the placenta showed severe hemorrhaging. When I was reinstated to the department, I submitted doctor's notes stating that I could not work and that when I was out of the house, even for a doctor's appointment, I had to be in a wheelchair.

The department, as they normally do, demanded that I come in to the clinic for an examination. On one of those occasions when I went to the clinic for an examination in the wheelchair accompanied by my husband, the department decided that I could, in fact, work and that they were putting me back to work.

I said "Okay, I will go back to work. Where shall I work?" They told my husband to push me into a room on the second floor of Jay Street which is police headquarters. I told my husband that he was not to do that. He was not an employee of the Transit Police Department. They had someone to push me into another room in a wheelchair where they sat and looked at me for another two or three hours.

Someone went to somebody else and decided maybe I should go back home. After this, although the District Attorney dropped the criminal charges against me, the Transit Police Department continued to pursue their charges.

I was again charged with disorderly conduct and—conduct unbecoming an officer. A total of 14 trial board hearings were scheduled. Nine of these trial board hearings were postponed by the Transit Authority, including one in which the hearing officer who lived in Virginia was unable to get a helicopter flight up to New York.

A total of five hearings were actually held. The first four were on the part of the department. One of those hearings was even held in my absence when my son had been attacked and his wrist had been severed the night before.

I was sitting in the hospital while he was undergoing microsurgery to have his wrist attached and the department refused to postpone the hearing that day.

After that, they gave me one day for hearings to present my side of the case. Two days before that date, my witness, the only witness that I had who was not known to me prior to this incident, had to go South for her father's funeral. They refused to postpone the hearing or set a later date for her to testify. As a result, I was terminated.

Let me just go back and give you a little bit of facts. Fact number one: When I had charges filed against me, I was placed on suspension without pay. At the same time, there was a white police officer who was undergoing his second allegation of rape, and yet he was suspended with pay. With pay means that you simply stay home, but you receive your full paycheck.

Fact number two: I had successfully passed the sergeant's exam and was near promotion. This, I believe, is a problem which the department feared.

Fact number three: There are white police officers who are known to have had more than 30 departmental derelictions and more than five trial board hearings and multiple civilian complaints, and these officers were never terminated.

Fact: I had three departmental derelictions prior to this one. The first was for being off post, meaning I was standing at the top of the subway stairs. The second one was for silver plating my off-duty weapon. The third one was for improperly reporting out sick. When I told them that I was unable to walk the five or six blocks to a different post at midnight because I was pregnant, I was wearing a police officer shirt, no shield, no weapon.

They refused to provide me with transportation. I told the sergeant then I would have to call in sick. I was not refusing the assignment, it was just that I could not walk to the assignment under those conditions. I had never had a trial board hearing before that time or any civilian complaints.

Fact: As of June 1, 1988, I was terminated from the Transit Police Department based on those allegations.

In conclusion, what I am trying to say is that no one here is safe. We are all subject to discrimination and these racist acts that are continuously going on within the police departments. It is not just affecting us as police officers, but it is affecting us as civilians.

My kids were traumatized by this. We have no immunity. We are like people with AIDS. We are severely, immunely depressed. Unless we do something about this vicious cycle of racism that is going on within the police departments here in the United States of America, we too will perish as people with AIDS.

Thank you. I was four months pregnant at the time of the incident.

Chairman OWENS. Thank you very much.

Mr. SURGEON. I have one more person.

Chairman OWENS. One more person?

Mr. SURGEON. Yes, Brother Tyler.

Chairman OWENS. We are a little pressed for time. Mr. Tyler, you may proceed, but try to confine your statement to five minutes. We would also appreciate the submission of your statement in writing.

STATEMENT OF RANDOLPH TYLER, JR.

Mr. TYLER. Good morning, Congressman Owens and panel. I am here to basically rehash what Ms. Boddie stated today concerning the disciplinary procedures of the New York City Transit Police Department.

On March 11, 1993, I presented to my sergeant a grievance letter that was made up of charges on a supervisor within my unit. The letter was then given to the captain.

The captain brought us all into his office and spoke with us concerning this grievance letter.

At that time, it was found out that I had written the grievance letter. After the sergeant found out that I had written it, I was overly supervised and consequently given a couple of disciplinary actions against me.

The first was sleeping in a transit police facility. The others, failure to sign in the command and control log, failure to have a radio on monitor calls, failure to make full and accurate entry book entries on and off duty.

Regarding the first charge, I was on meal and I wasn't sleeping in the facility at all. In fact, I was cramming for an exam I was taking at Saint Joseph College.

With reference to the failure to sign into the command and control log, nobody in the unit or indeed the district that I worked in ever signed in because of being in a specialized unit.

In terms of the failure to have the radio on monitor calls, I was on meal at that time.

For those charges, I was given 10 days suspension. While trying to effect an arrest two weeks after that, I was dragged by a cab and my radio was flung from my hand. I was given another five-day suspension time. I arrested the cab driver, but because my radio was flung from my hand, I lost more time.

All together, to make a long story short, I lost about $2,000 because I wrote a grievance letter against the sergeant. This practice is a common practice in the Transit Police Department.

They want African-American police officers to be seen, not heard. If we speak out against a supervisor or have anything to say about a certain event, we are looked at as militants, rabble-rousers. We should be happy to have a job.

It is frustrating for the new recruits coming in the department, because they feel they don't have any say. Being a field training officer, I encounter the new recruits when they come out of the academy. Many of them want to quit their job after two or three months in the department.

With encouragement from me and other African-American field officers, we try to keep these new officers on the job.

So I just hope that this committee can address the problems that African-American officers are having, so that African-American officers can walk with their heads up high, not having to always look down or behind our backs all the time because we say something or speak out about something.

I have 10 years on the job and during those 10 years, I have seen African-American officers have nervous breakdowns and just completely—just lose it.

These are fine men and women who came into the department with degrees, with high expectations of making a difference, but a difference after a couple of years seems non-reachable, you know.

I just hope that during my next 10 years I can help the Transit Police Department fight the crime in the subways. That is all I came here for: to help fight crime in the subway and to help the city. As African-American officers, we just should be thankful we have a job.

I hope that this committee can help African-American officers walk with their heads up high.

Thank you very much.

84-118 - 94 - 2

Chairman OWENS. I want to thank all of our witnesses.

The purpose of the testimony is to go that additional step. Previous investigations by governmental units have mostly focused on the very serious problem of recruitment and the fact that the number of minorities in the classes in academies, the minorities that started the process, was always very low. They have not focused much on questions related to retention, which means examining some of the issues that you have brought up in great detail, such as harassment and disrespect. One term—disparity in punishment—you have used is a very important phrase—disparity in punishment, meaning a double standard, which is harassment.

That leads to a situation where some of the very best are drummed out of the police corps. Most paramilitary organizations have the ability to do that because they don't have objective standards; they do have a lot of power, which is in the hands of supervisors who operate in very subjective ways.

We think that law enforcement units across the country can be greatly improved; that they could establish more objective standards for evaluations, for meting out punishment, and for promotions. The fact that it has not been done, is because it is not to the advantage of the majority. The old boy networks which run these paramilitary organizations, protect people; you can do nothing wrong if you are approved by the old boy network. That is not the way to run public agencies that are vital in the enforcement of laws which affect the lives of all citizens.

I have one or two questions and then I will yield to Mr. Payne.

Mr. Smith, has there been any action taken by the new administration in New Jersey which indicates that this problem is recognized and there is going to be some new approach taken in the New Jersey State Troopers?

Mr. SMITH. The New Jersey State Police has a habit of producing a lot of paperwork. A lot of their policies about harassment and the type of things that they will not tolerate, are put forth on paper, but in fact, it is business as usual and absolutely nothing has changed.

The same people are causing problems. Due to certain people in the rank structure, none of these people have been moved around or transferred to other locations. Nothing has been done as of this point.

Chairman OWENS. That is a pattern we see across the country; the top command, the mayors, the governors have the right language. They have the equal opportunity officers, all the trappings, but don't bother to deal with the rank and file and the kind of treatment they get from supervisors and middle management areas. That is a pattern that we found in all the agencies.

Ms. Lilly-Elmore, the statements that you made and the kind of details that you offered, will be invaluable as we pursue this effort.

The Equal Employment Opportunity Commission, as you know, has jurisdiction only over agencies which are receiving Federal funds. Some of our State police departments and cities receive some Federal funds, so they fall under the Equal Employment Opportunity Commission.

In addition, the Justice Department has jurisdiction over any kind of discrimination actions within municipal or State or governmental agencies. So it is our hope that we will push both of these entities, not just EEOC, but the Justice Department as well, to take a more vigorous approach to weeding out discrimination and examining the impact and effect of discrimination in law enforcement agencies.

Mr. Surgeon, of course, your details and your very personal notes on the pattern that led to your career being very much truncated and limited because of discrimination, are also quite valuable. The testimony of Ms. Boddie-Carter was another example of a concrete personal experience that is outrageous and could only happen in a very intensely racist atmosphere.

The situation has to be far worse than any of us could imagine if a person could be forced to go through that experience, but especially for a police officer to be forced to go through that experience after the charges are dropped and to be discharged by the Transit Authority. This is the kind of case we would like to pursue in greater detail to find out why the higher-ups did not pursue it in a way which would give justice to Ms. Boddie-Carter.

I yield to Mr. Payne for comments and questions.

Mr. PAYNE. Thank you very much.

Trooper Smith, in addition to there being a new governor, there is a new Superintendent of State Police also?

Mr. SMITH. That is correct, sir.

Mr. PAYNE. What is his name?

Mr. SMITH. Colonel Carl Williams.

Mr. PAYNE. He has been with the organization right along?

Mr. SMITH. That is correct.

Mr. PAYNE. In your opinion, have there been any real substantive changes in the procedure of the New Jersey State Police operation even though we have heard pronouncements?

Mr. SMITH. The problem is they have the ability to do whatever they want at any time they want to. That is what they don't want to change.

What they would rather change is their ability to say we have 20 percent promotions that are black people or something to that effect. When they do that, they just grab people and say "You are promoted. You are promoted. You are promoted. How many is that? Is that 20? That is good."

We want a fair system in which we don't need you as a boss to have to grab us and say "Okay, you are promoted." We want to get it on our own merit, not because you said so, because you need two more black people to fill a quota this week. We want to be able to put our record on the table, with our education, our degrees, and get promoted. That is what we want.

They won't do that because they want to have the power to keep you in your place by holding promotions and transfers and assignments over your head. If you speak out, they crush you like a bug and that is the way they are.

Mr. PAYNE. So in your opinion, they still have a double standard for African-American people, Hispanic men and women, people that they prefer not to be State troopers?

Mr. SMITH. Absolutely. Nothing has changed.

Mr. PAYNE. I understand that since late 1993, New Jersey State Police officers have to have a college degree; is that correct?

Mr. SMITH. That is correct, sir. You need a college degree to get into the State police.

Mr. PAYNE. It is noble to want to have very qualified people, I suppose, but have you seen or to your knowledge know whether that practice has mitigated against African-Americans becoming State troopers and do you think that perhaps since the job market is tight, especially around New Jersey and the Northeast, that maybe a plan would be to make the qualifications more strict where you know that you may have less African-American college graduates? Let's make that a criteria and that could be one of those mechanisms—what do you think about that?

Mr. SMITH. No doubt that is exactly what is going on. The State police are saying that this last class, the most people in the history of the State police that were minorities, took the examination and they were proud of the fact that so many minorities actually took the test. They forgot to tell you after all that was done how many actually got into the academy.

As of now, there are three African-Americans in the academy out of 158 people, which is the least amount of African-Americans that I can recall in my career, which is about 13 years. This would be the first class after the implementation of that college degree requirement; all of a sudden we are back to 1974.

Mr. PAYNE. Let me ask the New York City Police—Ms. Lilly-Elmore, what police agency are you with?

Ms. LILLY-ELMORE. I am not. I am with the New York City Correction Department.

Mr. PAYNE. I was going to ask a question about the new commissioner in New York.

Thank you. I have no other questions.

Chairman OWENS. I want to thank the members of the panel. We will certainly welcome any additional facts or written testimony you would like to submit in the next 10 days.

Our next panel consists of Officer Paula White-Ruiz, New York City Police Department; Officer Eric Sanders of the New York City Police Department; Sergeant Grace Ridley, President of the Guardians Association, New York City Police Department; and Osvaldo Rodriguez, Harbor Unit, New York City Police Department.

We will take a three-minute recess while you are getting situated.

[Brief recess.]

Chairman OWENS. We will resume the hearing.

We will begin with the testimony of Officer White-Ruiz, New York City Police Department.

STATEMENT OF PAULA WHITE-RUIZ, NEW YORK CITY POLICE DEPARTMENT

Ms. WHITE-RUIZ. Committee on Education and Labor, gentlemen and ladies, ever since I can remember, I wanted to become a policewoman. For years I had been listening to people complain about all the society ills and therefore I was determined to make a difference for myself, family, friends and neighbors. I was going to help create a better world to bring up my children.

So I entered the police academy to embark on a career path expectation in which I diligently and seriously undertook my training. On the day I graduated from the police academy, I prayed and hoped that I could make a difference. I had pride in myself and believed that together with my fellow police officers, we could make a difference.

My hopes came to a startling halt when only two weeks later, on January 28, 1988 while assigned to the 66th Precinct during a 4–to–12 tour, Police Officer Ward and I were instructed to investigate a 911 call regarding an unconscious male. When we arrived Police Officer Ward decided that he wanted to check for foul play because the door to this unconscious male's living quarters was open.

At the time, in accordance with my training, I requested the sergeant to respond. Police Officer Ward continued to search the premises, and we discovered money in the male's pocket. Ward commented "There goes another voucher," and he put the money back in the pocket.

Shortly thereafter, Ward asked me to leave the scene and retrieve his memo book from the auto. When I returned, I was locked out of the premises and had to wait for another apartment dweller to let me in. Momentarily, I returned to guard the body with P.O. Ward.

The sergeant arrived. He proceeded to search the male, but found no money other than some change. I informed the sergeant that earlier the DOA had paper money and that now it had disappeared. When the sergeant made a direct inquiry into this matter, Police Officer Ward denied that there had been any money in the pants.

That moment changed my life. I had come forward and reported an incident involving an allegation of misconduct of a fellow officer. I did so because I felt then, as I do now, that the reporting of this incident concerned a matter of public importance relating to public safety and good order.

If I did not report the incident, I knew that not only would I have been in violation of my oath of office, but that my ethics and morals would be compromised. I also knew, as did my fellow officers, that I would have been subject to disciplinary charges if I failed to report this incident.

I learned in the academy training that the act of reporting incidents of misconduct by members of the force, such as this incident, was a commendable, exemplary act deserving of recognition as good police work and I knew that such recognition had been accorded to other police officers.

The academy training also stressed that any officer meeting such high standards, reporting an allegation of an act of misconduct by a fellow officer, would be able to transfer to another command and be protected from retaliation while there. Therefore, I expected to be protected from retaliation and harassment. However, it was, and is still today, an unauthorized tradition in the New York City Police Department that police officers should not report acts of misconduct by fellow officers.

This tradition is sometimes referred to as the blue wall of silence and is viewed in some measure as a distorted act of camaraderie.

Upon my return to the 66th Precinct, Captain Scaggnelli indicated that he would be leaving soon for a promotion and that if I wanted to stay, I could, but after he left, he could not be sure what would happen to me. I chose to go to 88th Precinct.

Captain Scaggnelli told me that Chief Radford instructed him to send me to the 90th precinct where Chief Radford could make sure that nothing happened to me. As a result of my reporting the act of misconduct by a fellow officer, there began a deliberate course of retaliation by members of the police department.

Moreover, my superior officers and oversight personnel, learning of this retaliation, deliberately permitted it to continue without any supervisory response against those engaging in that conduct.

On February 4, 1988, I was transferred to the 90th Precinct where I met PAA Lucy Amoutic, who stated that she knew I was coming before I got there. Due to my pregnancy, I was transferred to the DA Squad until October 1988.

In October 1988, I returned to the 90th Precinct where I was greeted by some police officers who indicated that they did not want anything to do with me because I was "a rat."

A female police officer told me that Police Officer Hardy told her not to speak to the new black girl because she was a rat. Later, I began to see little notes on my locker saying "Rat and Black Bitch."

I received anonymously in the mail a copy of the personnel order stating that Police Officer Ward had been dismissed as of September 21, 1988. I took the letter to the Field Internal Affairs Unit at the 79th Precinct. The captain stated that he would start an investigation.

Then I began to get strange phone calls at my mother-in-law's house and Sergeant Lynch and Detective Boyd placed a tap on the phone to investigate.

For reasons unknown, and upon information and belief, there was no action taken to rectify the situation, either by adequate police investigation, roll call instruction or sensitivity training, nor was any discernible disciplinary or supervisory action taken to address the situation.

My career had taken on a new dimension. I was now a rat, and in recognition and appreciation of my new status in the department, I was rewarded the following:

In December of 1988, while on foot post, I stopped a car and requested from central a name check on a male; central reported that there was something wrong with my radio—that it kept breaking up; two auxiliary officers approached and on their radio, I could hear that someone was cutting off my transmissions by keying down when I spoke.

I had the auxiliary officers do the name check, and the male was found to be wanted in New York and Florida for assault with a shotgun. Central then requested that a unit respond to the location to assist me. Central went through each sector, and each time the unit reported it was busy.

A housing police unit came to assist me at the scene and transported me and the male suspect to the precinct. Upon my arrival at the precinct, I reported to Lieutenant Robert P. Butler and asked him to stop the officers from keying down on my transmissions because if they did not want to come and assist me, someone else might want help.

Thereafter, I began to get post changes from sector to the Amstar strike and the garment strike.

On January 30, 1991, I had a conference with Sergeant James McDermott concerning the unfair treatment I had been receiving. He stated that when officers do not look out for their bosses, then bosses don't look out for them. He also stated that he heard that I had "ratted" on him.

I also complained to him about preferential treatment given to other members of the service and unfair treatment to me.

On February 5, 1991, I complained that I was always being assigned to the Daily News strike at roll call. Police Administrative Assistant, "PAA," Virginia Galaway, a civilian, stated that the detail had come in and she assigned it to me and P.O. Ariza. Later I was told by two persons that PAA Galaway stated that she was assigning me and P.O. Ariza to the Daily News strike because no one else wanted to work with us anyway.

On that same day, I spoke to Lieutenant Alverez concerning bias incidents going on in the precinct. Lieutenant Alverez indicated that he would monitor the roll calls.

He stated that when incidents occur, it usually takes time to change, especially when rumors are spread and that I should give it time to ease.

Later that day, I was told that the commanding officer, Inspector Neuwirth, ordered that P.O. Ariza and I should not receive any more Daily News detail for the time being. However, other members of the service still continued to receive preferential treatment.

On March 21, 1991, I called Police Officer Joyce Hall of the 89th Precinct Brooklyn North Equal Employment Office, and told her that I had requested several interviews for Assignment to CPOP and that each time I was informed by Lieutenant Joseph Heffernan or Sergeant Vincent Marra that there were no openings.

Two days later, I found out that someone else, with less time than I had, was assigned to the position. It became evident that no matter what I did, I was continually being assigned the worst possible details.

Other officers, newly assigned, were put ahead of me, regardless of my seniority.

On March 22, 1991, P.O. Ariza and I were removed from our sector and assigned to foot post, which was not in accordance with seniority expectations.

On April 7, 1991, I spoke to Sergeant Vincent Marra about assignment to CPOP and was told that there were no openings. Just two days later, I found out that the post was given to someone else. There was another position open for school scooter that was posted and the requirement was to be scooter qualified, which I was. I applied for it and later found out that it was assigned to another officer who was not scooter qualified.

On September 13, 1991, I was informed by PAA Virginia Gallaway that she would have to remove me and P.O. Eheresman out of the car because P.O. Zimmerman had more time than we did "as per P.O. Zimmerman."

On September 14 and 18 of 1991, someone scratched my car on spite.

On April 12, 1992, I requested the opening in the CPOP and was told by Sergeant Marra that he did not know about it.

On April 16, 1992 I sought the help of the Office of Equal Employment Opportunity, a unit within the police department, and spoke to P.O. O'Connell and was given Log No. 108.

I was advised to call the Policeman's Benevolent Association directly. I also spoke with Lieutenant Harris about employee relations at the 77th Precinct. Lieutenant Harris stated that it was up to the commanding officer to decide what openings I could fill.

P.O. Santangelo of OEEO, called and stated that because the complaint of harassment was not bias-related, I should consult with the PBA or the Legal Bureau, and that at the time I was called a "Black Bitch," I should have called the OEEO. I believe that I was further retaliated against for going to Employee Relations.

On May 28, 1992 when I sought the help of OEEO, I was told by this office that there is no unit that handles whistleblowing complaints.

In the month of June of 1992, I once again applied for another opening. This position was in summons, and once again it was given to another police officer. I inquired of Lieutenant Dumbar why I was denied this opening. He screamed into the phone and said that he did not have to answer to me.

Unfortunately, my family experienced a hardship. Again, I requested most earnestly for other positions for which I not only had seniority in the department, but was trained and qualified. These positions were given to other members of the department who were not as trained or qualified and were on the force for substantially less time than I had been.

As a final attempt to resolve my unfortunate situation, I applied for an interview, in writing, on December 1992 with Police Commissioner Raymond Kelly, but to no avail. I was never given the interview.

Today, the retaliation and humiliation continues unabated as Police Commissioner William Bratton, who has personal knowledge of my situation, has joined in the ranks and stands by in silence.

I believe that there is no better way to signify my heartfelt humiliation and embarrassment for myself and fellow officers than by offering this committee copies of photographs of the men's latrine in the 90th Precinct.

For your reference, and as part of my testimony here today, I would like to read to you some of the sayings that have appeared:

"CCRB forms" with an arrow pointing to a toilet and a rat with my name appearing in the upper left-hand corner.

"Ariza sucks white Ruiz cock" in the outline of the R for rat.

"Let's face it. Ariza is testifying in favor of a known felon. His testimony is against two of our fellow officers. You figure it out."

"Ariza has two fathers."

"W.O. for P.O. Ariza tried to lock up a cop, a sergeant, in the 60th Precinct."

A male genital organ in relation to the above; "rats: Ariza, White-Ruiz, church, and the men's latrine."

Sharon Konits, my lawyer, contacted Judge Sotomayer to state that in our view, the graffiti in the men's latrine at the 90th Precinct was illegal, discriminatory, and a hate crime.

We requested that the court order the graffiti be memorialized and then eradicated. Internal Affairs Bureau had them quickly eradicate the graffiti by whitewashing the walls and had in effect destroyed evidence that was to be presented without permitting my lawyer the opportunity to personally view it and record the graffiti.

We are fortunate that the Court ordered that we be given all of the pictures that were recorded. As you will note, I added amateur photos that were taken by another officer that will depict in better detail what the graffiti additionally stated.

This graffiti was known to exist throughout the precinct and was in fact tolerated and left standing so that I and other officers would know that I was a rat.

I would like to end by saying that even though for the past eight years, I have been subjected to extreme humiliation and fear for my personal safety and the well-being of my family, given the same set of circumstances over again, I would not sacrifice my integrity, honesty and pride to be part of the blue wall of silence.

Thank you.

[The prepared statement of Ms. White-Ruiz follows:]

Committe on Education and Labor, Gentlemen and Ladies:

Ever since I could remember, I, Paula White Ruiz wanted to become a police woman. For years I had been listening to people complain about all of society's ills and therefore, I was determined to make a difference for myself, family, friends and neighbors. I was going to help create a better world to bring up children. So I entered the Police Academy, to embark on a career path expectation in which I diligently and seriously undertook my training. On the day I graduated the Police Academy, I prayed and hoped that I could make a difference. I had pride in myself and believed that together with my fellow police officers we could make the difference.

My hopes had come to startling halt when only two weeks later, on January 28, 1988, while assigned to the 66 Precinct during a 4:00 p.m. to 12:00 a.m tour, Police Officer Ward and I were instructed to investigate a 911 call regarding a white unconscious male. When we arrived, PO Ward decided that he wanted to check the scene for foul play because the door to this unconscious male's living quarters was opened. At this time, in accordance with my training, I requested that the Sergeant respond.

PO Ward continued to search the premises when he discovered money in the male's pocket. Ward then commented "there goes another voucher" whereby he put the money back in the pocket. Shortly thereafter, Ward ask me to leave the scene and retrieve his memo book. When I returned, I was locked out of the premises and I had to wait for another apartment dweller to let me in. Momentarily, I returned to guard the body with PO Ward. When the Sgt. arrived he proceeded to search the male, but found no money other than some change. I informed the Sgt. that earlier the DOA had paper money and that now it disappeared. When the Sergeant made a direct inquiry into this matter, PO Ward denied that there had been any money in the pants.

That moment had changed my life. I had come forward and reported an incident involving the alleged misconduct of a fellow officer. I did so because, I felt then as I do now that the reporting of this incident concerned a matter of great public importance, relating to public safety and good order. If I did not report the incident, I knew that not only would I have been in violation of my oath of office, but that my own ethics and morals would be compromised. I also knew as did my fellow officers that I to would have been subject to disciplinary charges if I failed to report this incident. I learned in academy training that the act of reporting incidents of misconduct by members of the force, such as this incident, was a commendable, exemplary act deserving of recognition, as good police work, and I know that such recognition has been accorded to other police officers. The academy training also stressed that any officer meeting such high standard (reporting an alleged act of misconduct by a fellow officer) would be able to be transferred to another command and also be protected from retaliation while there. Therefore, I expected to be protected from retaliation and harassment.

However, it was and is still today an unauthorized tradition in the New York City Police Department, that police officers should not report acts of misconduct of fellow officers. This tradition is sometimes referred to as the "blue wall of silence" and is viewed in some measure as a distorted act of comradely.

Upon my return to the 66th Precinct, Captain Scaggnelli indicated that he would be leaving soon for a promotion and that if I wanted to stay I could, but after he left, he could not be sure what would happen to me. I chose to go to the 88th Precinct. Captain Scaggnelli told me that Chief Radford instructed him to send me to the 90th Precinct, where Chief Radford could make sure that nothing happened to me.

As a result of my reporting the act of misconduct of a fellow officer, there began a deliberate course of retaliation by members of the police department. Moreover, my superior officers and oversight personnel, learning of this retaliation deliberately permitted it to continue without any supervisory response against those engaging in that conduct.

On February 4, 1988, I was transferred to the 90th Precinct and where I met PAA Lucy Amoutic, who stated that she knew I was coming before I got there. Due to my pregnancy, I was transferred to the DA Squad until October 1988. In October, 1988, I returned to the 90th Precinct where I was greeted by some police officers who indicated that they did not want anything to do with me because I was "a rat." A female police officer told me that Police Officer Hardy told her not to speak to the new black girl because she was a rat. Later, I began to see little notes on my locker saying "Rat **and Black Bitch".**

I started to received anonymously in the mail, a copy of the personnel order stating that Police Officer, Ward had been dismissed as of September 27, 1988. I took the letter to the Field Internal Affairs Unit at the 79th Precinct. The Captain stated that he would start an investigation. Then I began to get strange phone calls at my mother in law's house and Sergeant Lynch and Detective Boyd placed a tap on the phone to investigate. For reasons unknown, and upon information and belief, there was no action taken to rectify the situation either by adequate police investigation, roll call instruction or sensitivity training nor was any discernible disciplinary or supervisory action taken to address the situation.

My career had taken on a new dimension. **I was now a RAT!!!** and in recognition and appreciation of my new status in the department I was rewarded by the following:

- In December of 1988, while on foot post I stopped a car and requested from central a name check on a male; central reported that there was something wrong with my radio--that it kept breaking up; two auxiliary officers approached and on their radio I could hear that someone was cutting off my transmissions by keying down when I spoke. I had the auxiliary officers do the name check, and the male was found to be wanted in New York and Florida for assault with a shotgun. Central then requested that a unit respond to the location to assist me. Central went through each sector and each time the unit reported it was busy. A Housing Police unit came to assist me at the scene and transported me and the male suspect to the precinct. Upon my arrival at the precinct, I reported to Lieutenant Robert P. Bultler and asked him to stop the officers from keying down on my transmissions and that if they did not want to come and assist her, someone else might want help;

- Thereafter, I began to get post changes from sector to the Amstar strike and the garment strike;

- On January 30, 1991, I had a conference Sergeant James McDermott, concerning the unfair treatment I had been receiving. He stated that when officers do not look out for their bosses, then bosses don't look out for them. He also stated that he heard that I had "ratted" on him. I also complained to him about preferential treatment given to other members of the service and unfair treatment to me;

- On February 5, 1991, I complained that I was always being assigned to the Daily News strike at roll call. Police Administrative Assistant "PAA", a civilian, Virginia Galaway stated that the detail had come in and she assigned it to me and P.O. Ariza. Later I was told by two persons that PAA Galaway stated that she was assigning me and P.O. Ariza to the Daily News strike because no one else wanted to work with us anyway. On that same day I spoke to Lieutenant Alverez concerning bias incidents going on in the precinct. Lieutenant Alverez indicated that he would monitor the roll calls. He stated that when incidents occur it usually takes time to change, especially when rumors are spread and that I should give it time to ease. Later that day, I was told that the Commanding Officer, Inspector Neuwirth ordered that PO Ariza and I should not receive any more Daily News detail for the time being. However, other members of the service still continued to receive preferential treatment;

- On March 21, 1991, I called Police Officer Joyce Hall of the 89th Precinct Brooklyn North Equal Employment Officer, and told her that I had requested several interviews for assignment to C.P.O.P. and that each time I was informed by Lieutenant Joseph Heffernan or Sergeant Vincent Marra that there were no openings. Two days later I found out that someone else with less time than I had was assigned to the position. It became evident that no matter what I did, I was continually being assigned the worst possible details. Other officers newly assigned were put ahead of me, regardless of my seniority;

- On March 22, 1991, P.O. Ariza and I were removed from our sector and assigned to foot post, which was not in accordance with seniority expectations;

- On April 7, 1991, I spoke to Sergeant Vincent Marra, about assignment to C.P.O.P. and was told that there were no openings. Just two days later, I found out that the post was given to someone else. There was another position open for school scooter that was posted and the requirement was to be scooter qualified, which I was. I applied for it and later found out that it was assigned to another officer who was not scooter qualified;

- On September 13, 1991, I was informed by PAA Virginia Gallaway, that she would have to remove me and P.O. Eheresman out of the car because P.O. Zimmerman had more time than we did "As Per P.O. Zimmerman";

- On September 14 and 18th of 1991, someone scratched my car on spite;

- On April 12, 1992, I requested the opening in the C.P.O.P. and was told by Sergeant Marra that he did not know about it.

- On April 16, 1992, I sought the help of the Office of Equal Employment Opportunity (OEEO), a unit within the police department and spoke to P.O. O'Connell, and was given Log No. 108. I was advised to call the Policeman's Benevolent Association (PBA), direct; I also spoke with Lieutenant Harris about employee relations at the 77th Precinct. Lieutenant Harris stated that it was up to the commanding officer to decide what openings I could fill. P.O. Santangelo of OEEO, called and stated that because the complaint of harassment was not bias related, I should consult with the PBA or the Legal Bureau; and that at the time I was called a "Black Bitch", I should have called the OEEO. I believe that I was further retaliated against for going to Employee Relations.

- On May 28, 1992 when I sought the help of OEEO. I was told by this office that there is no unit that handles **"whistle blowing complaints."**

- In the month of June of 1992, I once again applied for another opening. This position was in summons and once again it was given to another individual police officer. I inquired why I was denied this opening to Lt. Dunbar. He screamed into the phone and said that he did not have to answer to me.

- Unfortunately my family experienced a hardship and again I requested most earnestly for other positions in which I not only had seniority in the department for but was trained and qualified. These positions were given to other members of the department who were not so trained or qualified and were on the force for substantially less time than I had been.

As a final attempt to resolve my unfortunate situation, I applied for an interview in writing on December 1992 with Police Commissioner, Raymond Kelly, but to no avail. I was never given the interview. Today, the retaliation and humiliation continues unabated as the Police Commissioner William Bratton who has personal knowledge of my situation has joined in the ranks as he stands by in silence.

I believe that there is no better way to signify my heart felt humiliation and embarrassment for myself and fellow officers than by offering this committee copies of photographs of the mens latrine in the 90 precinct. For your reference and as part of my testimony here today I would like to read to you some of the sayings that have appeared:

- C.C.R.B. FORMS WITH AN ARROW POINTING TO A TOILET AND A RAT WITH MY NAME APPEARING IN THE UPPER LEFT HAND CORNER;
- ARIZA SUCKS WHITE-RUIZ COCK IN THE OUTLINE OF THE R FOR RAT
- LETS FACE IT ARIZA IS TESTIFYING IN FAVOR OF A KNOWN FELON. HIS TESTIMONY IS AGAINST TWO OF OUR FELLOW OFFICERS. YOU FIGURE IT OUT;
- ARIZA HAS TWO FATHERS;
- W.O. FOR PO ARIZA TRIED TO LOCK UP A COP ... A SGT. IN THE 60 PCT.
- A MALE GENITAL ORGAN IN RELATION TO THE ABOVE;
- RATS:ARIZA WHITE-RUIZ CHURCH; AND
- THE MENS LATRINE.

Sharon Konits, my lawyer contacted Judge Sotomayer to state that in our view the graffiti in the mens latrine at the 90 precinct was illegal, discriminatory, and a hate crime. We requested that the court order the graffiti be memorialized and then eradicated. Internal Affairs Bureau had then quickly eradicated the graffiti by white-washing the walls and had in effect destroyed evidence that was to be presented without permitting my lawyers the opportunity to personally view it and record the graffiti. We are fortunate for the Court ordered that we be given all of the pictures that were recorded. As you will note, I added amateur photos that were taken by another officer that will depict in better detail what the graffiti additionally stated. This graffiti was known to exist throughout the precinct and was in fact tolerated and left standing because I and other officers would know that I was a Rat.

I would like to end by saying that even though for the past eight years, I have been subjected to extreme humiliation and fear for my personal safety and well being of my family, that given the same set of circumstances over again, I would not sacrifice my integrity, honesty and pride to be part of the blue wall silence.

Thank you.

Chairman OWENS. Thank you.
Officer Eric Sanders.

STATEMENT OF OFFICER ERIC SANDERS, NEW YORK CITY POLICE DEPARTMENT

Good morning to Hon. Major R. Owens, Chairman of the congressional Subcommittee on Select Education and Civil Rights and the other members of the committee.

My name is Eric Sanders. I am 29 years old and I am a member of the New York City Police Department, Shield No. 23973, and currently assigned to the 113th Precinct, Uniformed Patrol.

I have lived in New York City all my life. I graduated from Andrew Jackson High School. I attended Norwich University, Northfield, Vermont. I am currently awaiting the fall semester to reregister, so I can finish studying criminology and ultimately pursue my law degree.

I was appointed to the New York City Police Department on January 26, 1988. I was assigned to the Recruit Training School, where I achieved a cumulative average of 3.545, which is equivalent to an A average. I was named most likely to succeed in my company by a vote of 88 to 29.

After successfully completing my classroom course of study, I was assigned to Field Training Unit No. 17. On January 3, 1989, I was assigned to the 101st Precinct in Far Rockaway, Queens.

I was assigned to the Recruitment Unit several times during the 1992 and 1993 calendar year. On January 19, 1994, I was assigned to my current command, the 113th Precinct.

I have been a member of the Guardians Association for 6½ years, where I served three years as a delegate. I currently hold the position of First Vice President.

During my career, I have received department recognition in the grade of Excellent Police Duty, five; and Meritorious Police Duty, two.

I received numerous letters from the community for my dedicated service. I have never caused a defendant an injury by the use of force.

I have never been involved in any radio car accidents. I received the lowest amount of complaints, five, of which none were substantiated.

I have always had the reputation of being a sharp and active police officer. I have been out sick only one time in 6½ years. I have always had the reputation of being an honest and straight police officer.

During my years of service as a public servant, I have observed a police culture that is completely insensitive to the issue of racial diversity. From the time of my swearing in at Brooklyn Technical High School, I noticed the nepotism, cronyism, racism and sexism that permeates the entire department. I have personally witnessed the double standards applied during roll call. In the recruit training school, I noticed how some recruits were disciplined and others were given preferential treatment.

As an African-American, I am in the minority in several categories. Most obviously, African-Americans represent only 10 percent of the entire police force, with no meaningful representation within the Police Benevolent Association, no board members, and only three delegates that serve citywide.

Next, I am in the minority because I am one of a small number of officers who have spoken out against the inequities within the force. As a consequence, I have been unjustly harassed and harshly punished for such action.

When I was assigned to my first command, I began to notice how I was rated differently on my yearly evaluations, even though I was active, came to work fit for duty. Meanwhile, my counterparts were lazy, sometimes unfit for duty, et cetera, and they received the same rating as mine or higher. These same police officers received choice assignments. Meanwhile, with my spotless record at that time, I seemed to qualify for nothing.

On numerous occasions, I have heard my colleagues call residents of the African-American and Latino communities epithets such as animals, niggers, faggots, spics, et cetera. This behavior continues, no matter what socioeconomic background they come from. We are referred to as jungles.

The Patrolman's Benevolent Association does nothing to support African-American police officers who allege discriminatory practices, unprofessional or unethical conduct. Many times we are labeled as troublemakers and continue our careers unsupported by the various unions, such as the Sergeants' Benevolent Association, Lieutenants' Benevolent Association, and Superior Officers Council, despite their obligation to do so in accordance with collective bargaining agreements.

African-American police officers and detectives as of December 1993 make up 7.9 percent of males in the New York City Police Department, and approximately 4.6 percent females, averaging 12.5 percent total in the whole New York City Police Department.

I can give you a little history about myself.

My partner was assigned to a radio car unit. I was assigned with another police officer and my regular partner. We responded to a location in Far Rockaway, where there was a large disorderly group of people who were drunk, at approximately 7 a.m. At that time Sergeant Keith Bratwell, who was on patrol, came to the scene and we broke up people from fighting and tried to get them to go on about their way.

Sergeant Bratwell was walking around and saying "I can't believe these fucking spics." So I walked over to him and said, "Sarge, that was uncalled for." He looked at me and didn't say anything, and that started the whole thing with this harassment.

On June 15, 1991, I was assigned to a 1053, which is an accident, on 38th Street and the Rockaway Freeway. I observed a female in a car who looked like she might have been drinking. She crashed and totaled the car and ran into the fire hydrant.

I asked for her driver's license. She didn't have one. I gave her a test to make sure she was not intoxicated and I gave her a summons for not having a New York State driver's license. At that time, the sergeant told me I did not handle the job properly.

It turned out to be a police officer's wife, a police officer's car she was driving. I thought it ended there. The next day at roll call, a police officer who addressed the roll call stated, "If you don't know how to handle an accident, call the boss. If you don't have a driver's license in the State of New York, you should be issued a universal summons." So, I had handled the job properly.

That night when I came in, I found that my locker was still standing, but when I opened it, everything was shaken up and all the gun belts and garments were in the bottom of the locker. I spoke to my captain about it, but he offered no assistance to me.

On January 11, we responded to a 1034, which is a female assault, at 1302 Redfern Avenue, a housing development in Far Rockaway. Sergeant Engel pulled up alongside our radio car—I was with my regular partner, Police Officer Derek Avery; we were known as being very active, so everyone knew us—and said, "Are you finished?" I responded, no. He said "Well, there is central, the communication that gives us the jobs. They are holding a job in your sector." He wanted us to pick it up. I said, "Where are the other sectors?" We were the only ones responding back and forth with the precinct.

He said "Just pick up the job. You have left the location." I felt bad because the woman in back was African-American; she was from the projects and she was poor.

I have watched, during my whole career, how they treat people differently. If it were a white woman with blond hair and blue eyes, they would have asked "Do you need an ambulance? Do you have a description of the perpetrators?"

He might have put her in his car, but for the fact that she came from the projects. I grew up in the projects so I took offense to that.

He requested to speak to me after roll call. His two friends, sergeants, once they get there, start drinking and hanging out with the guys.

In another sector, Police Officer McNulty-Stile was holding a 1011, or ringing an alarm in a building, for approximately 45 minutes. It doesn't take 45 minutes to search and see if you can secure a building or if, in fact, the building was broken into.

He told me that he is the supervisor and I shouldn't tell him how to monitor the radio; "If the sectors aren't picking up their jobs, you should talk to them."

As I stated earlier, he did this in front of the switchboard located in the front as soon as you walk in the precinct, because the general public and police officers have to pass the desk officer before they can go to the back.

He said at that time, "If you don't respect me, I will teach you one way or another."

On 8/29, we had a car stopped between Plainview Avenue and Seacord Boulevard. I was working with the Star Right Protector Services. A white car driven by Steven Bennett was going northbound on 20th Street. He made a left turn through a red light. He had a friend in the car, sitting on the back lid because it was a convertible, and the music playing very loud. I stopped him and asked why he ran the red light. He told me "I have the same authority you have." Because he was a police officer, he was given that right by his agency so they could secure that property.

I explained to him that you can't run red lights, especially in a private car. "Are you chasing someone?" He said, "I don't care. I have the same authority as you and you can't stop me."

I asked for his driver's license, registration and insurance card. He got out of the car and started shouting at me. At that time, I requested the patrol supervisor who did not come to the scene. I gave Mr. Bennett a universal summons for disobeying a steady red light. I ran his name through night spin and came back with a warrant for burglary, second degree.

Since I spoke to Sergeant Babalaw a couple of days earlier and I knew they were looking for every little thing to get me, I didn't bring the guy in on this burglary warrant. It pretty much matched him, except for the Social Security number. But we all know that sometimes people change their Social Security number and date of birth.

I didn't bring him in. He probably was a wanted felon. He complained against me.

Sergeant Babalaw told my partner, "I don't know what is the matter with him, but you better get away from him because if you don't, you will go down with him."

He takes the complaint and investigates it, saying if I had extended a little more courtesy, maybe I wouldn't have gotten a complaint. He said I didn't follow procedures. He referred me to the patrol guide section to teach me how to issue summons.

Approximately two days later, September 1, I was involved in an arrest situation of a 1034, a female was assaulted with a sawed-off shotgun, and her husband fired one shot at her. I responded with my partner, Police Officer McNulty-Stile. Sergeant Engel was on the desk and Sergeant Babalaw on patrol.

We responded to the location. She told me, "My husband hit me with a sawed-off shotgun and fired a shot at me." We put her in the car, got a description, and started canvassing the neighborhood, at which time Police Officer McNulty-Stile said "We have a person under observation."

I said "Stand by. We will respond to the location," then I hear a radio transmission of "We have one under observation." I said "Stand by," because I didn't conduct a show-up, so we don't know if it is the right guy.

We get there and I asked what happened. They said "We don't want to talk. We are not going to court." I was stuck with the collar for the arrest because I was the recorder at the time and there is standard policy that started back—I don't when—that the recorder has to get stuck with the collar.

They bring the gentleman to the station house and I bring the woman to the hospital for treatment for her arm. I get back to station house and there is a log entry in the command log that I brought this gentleman in.

I started to have a conversation with Sergeant Babalaw, but he is angry at me for telling him not to call someone a spic.

I want to tell him that these guys will not tell me who stopped him; why no form was filled out, what they did and whether they, in fact, recovered the weapon legally from the guy.

He said "Go to the back." I processed the arrest and the next day he called internal affairs. There was an Internal Affairs investigation initiated on me. The Integrity Control Officer, who is a lieutenant most of the time in the precinct, approached me the next day.

He said, "Eric, Internal Affairs called me to ask what kind of cop you were, and I said you were a good cop." I said to myself, "what else could you say? I have been clean all these years. What else could you say?"

The investigation continued so I know they are trying to build a paper trail on me.

Next a woman in Far Rockaway complained that an eight-year-old kid alleges he was beat up by a security officer. I went to the scene and I immediately knew the apartment. It seems like you go to the same places over and over again. So I knew a little bit about the family history.

I interviewed the child and I asked the woman to come downstairs with me so I could interview the security officer and find out what happened. She said "No, I am going to send my 16-year-old daughter downstairs with you."

Meanwhile, there is a woman standing there who is her niece saying, "He is just mad because he wants to fuck me and I won't give him no pussy" and this kind of nonsense.

I go downstairs with the kid and I conduct this investigation. After talking to all parties, I concluded that the security officer did nothing wrong. I have witnesses that saw the incident and stated that he did nothing wrong. All he did was grab the kid and try to bring him upstairs.

I thought it was over, but the woman called in a complaint to the commander and said "If there were two white cops here, they would have arrested this man." Because he was black, she figured he could have been arrested and that would have furthered her civil suit. She wants to sue the corporation which runs the housing facility.

She called the desk officer, at the time, Sergeant McElvoy. I had the reputation if there was an arrest to be made, I would make the arrest. I was not known as dumping an arrest to get out of it.

Sergeant Babalaw is in the area of the desk officer and as soon as he heard the name, Sanders he took the phone from the other sergeant and says, "I will be right there."

He took a camera from behind the desk and did a beeline to the woman's house. There is nothing in civilian complaint that says anything about going to anyone's house to give them personal service with a camera. I could only surmise that because I was involved in it, he decided he was going to build more paper on me and try to hurt me with this.

He and Lt. Martin Hannish went to the woman's house and did an interview. They came back and took my partner into a separate room and asked about the complaint we made, which was harassment at that time. He ordered my partner to change it to Assault 3, endangering the welfare of a child. He asks, "How is it to work with Eric? Is he okay? Does he have a drinking problem? Is he a gambler?"

My partner said "I don't have a problem with him. He is a good cop." He told him, "A word to the wise: If you don't get away from him, you are going to go down with him."

He reopened the case and referred it to the Detective Squad. They looked at the case and said, "If Eric didn't make the arrest, that means there was no arrest to be made." I was known as an active police officer.

They went upstairs and talked to the detectives, trying to get them to pursue the case. The detectives interviewed all the parties and came to the same conclusion we came to; that there was no crime committed.

Lieutenant Hannish called one of his buddies, a captain at Detective Queens, and had him reopen the case. This went on for about four months. This case for assault or alleged assault generated 31 follow-ups, which is almost as much, if not more, than a homicide.

It was ultimately referred to the District Attorney's Office which found that there was no crime committed and closed it for harassment again.

They called another District Attorney, who was a bureau chief, and had him reopen it. Subsequently, they found that what we did was proper.

Needless to say, the civilian complaint that was filed against us should have been unfounded. Lieutenant Hannish took it upon himself to substantiate it, saying that while the conduct of Police Officers Sanders and Avery was not malicious, but because of their lack of ability and skills, et cetera, should have known that there was a crime and should have effected a summary arrest; that what we did was improper. They recommended that we be split up in 90 days.

The captain signed off on this. Meanwhile, I have 31 follow-ups to say we did everything properly. That is abuse of authority. After that, I made an EEO complaint. I went to the EEO and they told me I had no case.

I was given an evaluation by the same sergeant.

For 11 months out of 1991, I was rated as above and well above average. One month, I was rated below average by Sergeant Keith Babalaw. I thought I would be rated above average and I was rated "meets standards."

I will tell you a couple of comments he put here: "Community interaction, low." The area where we worked was the housing development and I spent 10 years of my life there. I knew everyone. As a matter of fact, they had street names for us, Batman and Robin, Starsky and Hutch, Black on Black, et cetera. We got along well there.

"Police interaction and notification, low. Police ethics integrity, low. Interpersonal skills, low. But highly competent, apprehension intervention."

If I was highly competent at apprehension intervention, don't you think common sense would dictate if there was a lawful arrest to be made, I would have made an arrest?

"Processing arrests, highly competent. Vouchering, highly competent. Clerical duties, highly competent. Appearance, highly competent. Special orientation, highly competent. Police officer is good, but he has a bad attitude." That is what they are telling me.

"Police officer at times is insensitive and indifferent to the resident of the community." What did he base this on? I have no idea because he didn't speak to anyone in the community.

"Does not always exchange pertinent information about incidents with his immediate supervisor." That is the operative word, "his."

"Has nothing to do with anyone else." It is personal.

"Prefers to use authoritative rather than persuasive methods to achieve results."

I never had to assault anyone. I don't have any abuse or complaints on my record for hitting anyone. I have chased people with Tech 9 machine guns, sawed-off shotguns. I was in the middle of a gunfight with 9-millimeter handguns and a 357, and never had to do that.

"Officer Sanders' performance in regard to control activity is above standards. However, he tries the patience of his supervisor through his reluctance to take directions, requiring direct orders by his rater. Police Officer Sanders does not take constructive criticism well."

You say all these good things about Police Officer Sanders, but meanwhile, you are saying that he has a bad attitude. It has nothing to do with work. It has to do with personality conflicts.

After that, I was summoned down to the Queens District Attorney's Office.

Chairman OWENS. Can you wrap it up?

Mr. SANDERS. I was summoned to the Queens District Attorney's Office. I had never been arrested or had any problems with the law. They tried to lock me up for perjury.

I went down on my own. I asked the lawyer, "Do I need a lawyer?" He says, "No." He asked me "Is the sergeant white?" I said, "yes." He quickly backed down and said "I don't want anything to do with this. I will send you for administrative trial."

I went for administrative trial. I had a Police Benevolent Association attorney, Pat O'Brien. I spent approximately 10 minutes with him on this case before I went to trial. I went to the trial room. We discussed the charges, went through a trial and the woman didn't have her facts together.

I got 30 days—perjury for this arrest. The sergeant was involved. The phone call was in. There was no way I was going to win this case. I was convicted and on a year's probation.

I told my lawyer, "Put in the paperwork. I want to appeal it." He says, "There is no law violation. Why do you want to appeal it? You should be happy you weren't fired."

I am appealing and now everyone is angry. This is ridiculous. I have watched, through my career, police officers who are drunk in the station house get caught by a duty captain. They should be suspended on the spot. They are not being suspended. They are being sent out to Long Island while the brothers and sisters are getting trumped up on charges because they have a problem with a sergeant. He doesn't like their attitude.

A police officer pulls out a gun in roll call. This police officer should be suspended. There is something wrong with him. They don't do anything to that police officer.

This goes on every day. Nobody is saying anything. Every day, brothers and sisters get burned by this nonsense system they think is fair. There is no such thing as fair. We are getting burned on nonsense.

When you look at the television, you see corrupt police officers. What do you see? You see black police officers. They are talking about lower standards and we are getting hired.

When they lower the standards, guess who gets hired? They get hired. We don't get hired. We were always passing the tests and had the qualifications, but they always screen us out. They say we are troublemakers; we are rabble-rousers. If they could have identified me through the system, they would have, but I have played the game. I know how it works.

They couldn't identify me if I didn't want them to, but now it is time for them to stop.

[The prepared statement of Mr. Sanders follows:]

Good Morning, to the Honorable Major R. Owens, Chairman of the Congressional Subcommittee on Select Education and Civil Rights and the other members of the committee.

My name is Eric Sanders, I am 29 years old and I am a member of the New York City Police Department, Shield No. 23973 and currently assigned to the 113th Precinct, Uniformed Patrol.

I have lived in New York City all my life. I graduated from Andrew Jackson High School. I attended Norwich University, Northfield Vermont. I am currently awaiting the fall semester to re-register, so, I can finish studying Criminology and ultimately pursue my law degree.

I was appointed to the New York City Police Department on January 26, 1988. I was assigned to the Recruit Training School, where I achieved a cumulative average of 3.545. I was voted most likely to succeed in my company 88-29. After successfully completing my classroom course of study I was assigned to Field Training Unit #17. On January 3, 1989, I was assigned to the 101st Precinct. I was assigned to the Recruitment Unit several times during the 1992 and 1993 calendar year. On January 19, 1994, I was assigned to my current command the 113th Precinct.

I have been a member of the Guardians Association for 6 1/2 years, where I served 3 years as a delegate. I currently hold the position of 1st Vice President.

During my career I have received Department Recognition in the grade of:

Excellent Police Duty	5
Meritorious Police Duty	2

I received numerous letters from the community for my dedicated service. I have never caused a defendant an injury by the use of force. I have received a low amount of Civilian Complaints, approximately five none of which were substantiated. I have always had the reputation of being a sharp and active Police Officer. I have been out sick only one time in 6 1/2 years. I have always had the reputation of being an honest and straight Police Officer.

During my years of service as a public servant, I have

observed a police culture that is completely insensitive to the issue of racial diversity. From the time of my swearing in at Brooklyn Technical High School I noticed the nepotism, cronyism racism and sexism that permeates the entire department. I have personally witnessed the double standards applied during roll call. In the Recruit Training School, I noticed how some recruits were disciplined and others were given preferential treatment.

As an African American, I am in the minority in several categories. Mostly obviously, African Americans represent only 10% of the entire police force, with no meaningful representation within the Police Benevolent Association: No Board members and only approximately 3 delegates that serve city-wide.

Next, I am in the minority because I am one of a small number of officers who have spoken out about against the inequities within the force. As a consequence, I have been unjustly harassed and harshly punished for such action.

When I was assigned to my first command, I began to notice how I was rated differently on my Yearly Evaluations. Even though I was active, came to work fit for duty etc. Meanwhile, my counterparts were lazy, sometimes unfit for duty etc, and they received the same rating as myself or higher. These same Police Officers received choice assignments. Meanwhile, with my spotless record at that time, I seemed to qualify for nothing.

On numerous occasions, I have heard my colleagues call residents of the African-American and Latino Communities epithets such as: animals, niggers, faggots, spices etc. This behavior continues, no matter what socio-economic background they come from. We are referred to as: jungles.

The Patrolman's Benevolent Association does nothing to support African-American Police Officers who allege discriminatory practices, unprofessional or unethical conduct. Many times we are labeled as trouble-makers and continue our careers unsupported by the various unions, despite their lawful obligation to do so in accordance with the collective bargaining.

African-American Police Officers and Detectives as of December 1993 (NYPD)

7.9%	Males	1939
4.6%	Females	1132
12.5%	Total	3071

Chairman OWENS. Sergeant Grace Ridley.

STATEMENT OF SERGEANT GRACE RIDLEY, PRESIDENT, GUARDIANS ASSOCIATION, NEW YORK CITY POLICE DEPARTMENT

Ms. RIDLEY. Thank you.

Good morning. I am Grace Ridley, President of the Guardians Association of the New York City Police Department. I would like to thank the members of the Committee of Education and Labor Subcommittee on Select Education and Civil Rights for the opportunity to address this body regarding discrimination.

Chairman OWENS. Excuse me, Sergeant Ridley. Congressman Payne will have to leave in a few minutes and he wanted to make a brief statement before he leaves.

Ms. RIDLEY. I have some questions for Congressman Payne, too.

Mr. PAYNE. You will have to put them in writing. I have to get back to New Jersey for a press conference that I have to attend.

I would just like to thank the officers for coming forth. As the Chairman said earlier, it certainly takes a great deal of courage for you to step forward and tell it like it is.

We will continue to hold hearings to try to get to the truth and try to reform this very important agency, the agency that is supposed to protect citizens and is supposed to be fair, because you represent the law. We know—whether it is in New Jersey or New York, whether it is in Pennsylvania or California—that there is a lot of racial discrimination and sexual discrimination within the agencies. We will continue to be vigilant, to hear testimony, to get the record straight so that hopefully we will be able to get the proper civil rights agencies of the Federal Government to do the right thing to turn around these organizations which have such a blatant history of racial discrimination.

I would like to thank you all again and thank the Chairman for continuing these hearings.

Chairman OWENS. Thank you.

Ms. RIDLEY. Before you leave, would you like me to answer your question about Commissioner Bratton? I can tell you that he is a tap dancer, definitely for the news media, and has not done anything for the African-Americans in the police department. We represent African-American civilians and police officers.

We have 8,000 civilians and 3,000 police officers and he had told me on a one-on-one that there are no African-Americans qualified to hold any of the top positions in the New York City Police Department. If that answers your question, sir——

Mr. PAYNE. It certainly does.

Ms. WHITE-RUIZ. That only proves that there is a battle to keep the status quo. That means that they are in and we are out.

We are always going to be on the outside looking in and I challenge you, both of you, to fix it. There is no way in hell that you are going to get those Irish and Italians out of office. This is a family-run organization.

It might be funded by the city, but the family runs it. We are just their lackeys, their tokens. As long as we have enough breath in our body to open our mouth, we will suffer and suffer. For seven long years, I have suffered immensely.

Chairman OWENS. I would like to remind you that Congressman Payne comes from Newark, New Jersey. You can't hold him responsible for correcting what happens here. However, in the process of correcting the pattern that we find throughout the whole country, we will be able to make corrections here. I am sure the pattern in New Jersey is no different from the pattern here.

Thank you again, Donald, for coming.

Sergeant Ridley.

Ms. RIDLEY. I would like to give statistics for the New York City Police Department as far as their personnel is concerned. We have 231 black sergeants, 67 black lieutenants, 1 black female captain, and we have 7 black—I should say captains and above—inspectors, deputy inspectors, deputy chiefs are all captains, but with appointed titles, and that is the number.

Out of a total of over 31,000 police officers, we have less than 3,500 African-Americans in the New York City Police Department. That is just police officers. We have just a little over 8,000 African-American civilians represented in our agency.

These are numbers as of February 28, 1994. These numbers are not any different from 20 years ago. We have not had an increase in the last 20 years.

Chairman OWENS. Are those contained in the original statement or additional——

Ms. RIDLEY. These are additional.

Chairman OWENS. Please submit those to us for the record.

Ms. RIDLEY. Due to short notice in receiving my invitation to this hearing, I am shocked—dismayed—but I am really appalled to think that in two days of notification, I can give you a accurate number of cases documented on blatant discriminatory practices and racism within the New York City Police Department.

There are several persons who would have been able to testify today and because of the lack of notice, of being treated like third-, fourth-, fifth-class citizens, we are appalled. There would probably be standing room only here right now had we had sufficient notification, because people are angry.

We do not like to be discriminated against and we have been doing that over and over and over again. I have only been president of this organization since January 1994, but I have been a member of the New York City Police Department for the last 12 years and discriminatory practices and racism have not gotten better; they have gotten worse.

The issues are: number one, residency. All persons hired for the New York City Police Department for the position of police officer should be New York City residents. We feel that they would be better suited as police officers if they lived within the New York City area. They have a vested interest in the city in which they live because they have family here and pay taxes here and they would be more responsible for the well-being of others.

Above all, the department would be more representative of the citizens of New York. Furthermore, according to the regulations, we are on duty 24 hours a day, including emergencies. They can call us out at any given hour because they have a riot somewhere, and we have to respond.

If we were responding to our own African-American communities, I think we would be more apt to handle the situation.

Discriminatory practices in hiring. There are currently four existing tests of candidates, No. 9006, 0079, 1007 and 1177, of which two have not yet been promulgated. Test 9006 will expire 10–94. Test 0079 will expire 3–95, and Test 0294 will expire 7–95.

The investigative practices in the Applicant Processing Division should be challenged and needs to be revamped. There should be more African-American medical doctors and psychologists employed by the department. This would probably ensure that fair and unbiased practices would be implemented.

Although there are only two African-Americans to head the medical and psychological units, they have contact with the candidates entering the department on a limited basis. There are no African-American psychologists who conduct interviews and tests for incoming candidates, nor are there any medical doctors or nurses to conduct medical examinations for candidates and cadets entering this department.

The African-American candidates are often discriminated against before they begin the investigation process. They are disqualified as soon as they walk through the door by their case investigators who are 90 percent white and have a biased opinion about African-Americans from their upbringing. They have limited contact with ethnic groups and tend to bring these prejudices with them to the agency.

African-American candidates are usually disqualified for: one, not being employed for two to three years; two, having babies out of wedlock; and three, the appeal process. These practices are deemed discriminatory for African-Americans, but valid reasons for white candidates.

As a police officer, you can acquire information from your investigator as to your position, pass or fail, on psychologicals from the investigator. In order to appeal the psychological process, you have to receive written confirmation from the department, which on average is nine months later, then they make some type of determination.

The timing almost excludes you from appealing because this process takes almost an additional year. The Department of Personnel has abdicated their responsibility in reference to the psychological appeals and in essence the police department is appealing itself.

At least 50 percent of the candidates have taken two or three examinations and could possibly be on two or three lists waiting to be hired. A true number of persons waiting to be hired is not available at this time. The reason the candidates are on different lists is that they have some type of insurance that will give them a second chance to be employed in case the list dies, their investigation is held over, medical or psychological or character investigations are being reviewed.

The appeal processes, as stated in the previous paragraph, is appalling. Investigators often carry approximately 150 to 200 cases per person. The possibility exists where the investigators may select the "cream puff" cases, which is the easiest cases possible with the least amount of work to pass through, and these cases are not those of African-American candidates.

The unit is understaffed; the investigators handle too many cases. In the New York City Police Department Cadet program, which is approximately 85 percent African-American, they are being screened out with the same biased practices in medical, psychological and character investigations even though they are initially qualified upon being a cadet.

During the last examination, No. 1177, there were 31,000 people who passed. That is an entire New York City Police Department. I can tell you today that out of those 31,000 people who passed that exam, approximately 2,000, maybe, will be hired, and that is at least eight years from now.

So if they were 29 to 35 years old—because our cutoff age is 35 years of age—they will not be hired even though they took this exam.

In addition, the investigation process is often an excruciating experience for African-Americans. They are humiliated, disrespected, and on numerous occasions told that they are wasting their time. This results in many African-Americans dropping out of the process.

The department lacks an adequate retention procedure, which is critical and crucial to African-American candidates. They have eliminated the retention part of the investigation process as far as the New York City Department is concerned.

We would propose that the Federal Government hold back Federal funds to law enforcement agencies throughout the country, especially New York City, dealing with education in law enforcement, until a full investigation is conducted on the procedures and policies of the New York City Police Department. Surely the discrimination practices are more sophisticated in that they have four existing lists and the Department of Personnel wants to be held accountable; we are trying to alleviate that process also.

The Department of Personnel is no good for the New York City Police Department because they weigh test scores or they make up their own rules when it comes to who passes, who fails, who gets hired and who doesn't get the job.

Per the testimony of Roger Ables, our past Guardians Association President and former Chief of Personnel O'Sullivan at the Equal Employment Practices Commission on March 1993, "African-American candidates are not as successful as majority candidates on the character investigations and psychological screening. African-American candidates also appear to discontinue processing at a higher rate than majority candidates. The combined effect results in a African-American appointment rate which is less than what is hoped for."

The historical perspective: In 1991, a study by the New York City RAND Institute entitled, "Majority Recruiting in the New York City Police Department" discussed issues relating to the attraction and retention of minority candidates.

According to the study, one major factor accounting for underrepresentation of minority group members is the high rate of attrition among applicants who passed the exam, but withdrew from the hiring process.

The study noted that this drop-out rate is higher among African-Americans than other ethnic groups. The limited employment of African-Americans as police officers in the New York City Police Department has been a subject of analysis for more than 20 years. Studies on this issue have focused on racial bias within the New York City Police Department and discriminatory hiring practices.

Gains in hiring have been attributed in large part to legal challenges in the discriminatory employment practices of the New York City Police Department. In 1979, the Guardians Association sued the city charging the city—charging the police department—excuse me—charging that the police Examination 8155 was discriminatory.

The court found that the same examination had a disparate impact on minorities. As a result, the city was directed to achieve a minority hiring ratio of 33 percent pending development of valid selection processes.

Again we find ourselves in the same situation fighting discriminatory practices, both in captain's and lieutenant's examinations, and a compromise and disparate impact on African-Americans on the sergeant's examination, New York City Police Department 1528.

In that compromise sergeant's examination, the Guardians Association, wrote to former Mayor Dinkins, at that time Mayor-elect Giuliani, Police Commissioner Kelly, and the new Police Commissioner Bratton, Internal Affairs Division, Department of Personnel, and the Department of Investigations. We have all this documented.

We told them on November 22, 1993, that this test had been compromised and four months to this date, April 21, a Housing Police Officer, Robert Temple, was arrested and charged with criminal possession of stolen property and other related charges; the officer was alleged to have in his possession the promotion examination of the New York City Police Department.

This arrest substantiates our accusations and allegations of the compromising of that examination. That is on record.

There are allegations of widespread cheating on the sergeant's examination and there was alleged to have been an arrest made, but Police Commissioner William Bratton continues to promote off this list of about 3,000 names, in which we can only identify 50 African-Americans.

The original allegation by the Guardians Association included a police administrative aide who allegedly removed the test from the test site on the Sabbath Observers day of the examination.

We have heard nothing relative to that allegation, but shortly thereafter, they started to make provisional appointments.

Promotions: Within the New York City Police Department, there are three grades in the detective rank and basically there are monetary increases: third-grade detective salary from police officer to sergeant; second-grade equivalent to a sergeant salary, and first-grade equivalent to a lieutenant salary.

We have African-Americans with a minimum of 20 years of service with the New York City Police Department, 16 years as a third-grade detective.

The New York City Police Department has recently set up a criteria for grade assignments within the last two years, but has not devised a plan to include African-Americans to be promoted prior to this criteria. So detectives with a third-grade assignment, mostly African-Americans, have no way to reach those standards of the 1990s and all the work of 16 years goes unrewarded.

The white officers who have relatives on the job, whether they be chiefs, inspectors, or captains, get placed on a grid and in a data-based system so that you cannot tell where you are or when you are going to get promoted.

These promotions are based on a panel decision and you are not told the results upon your interview of this process.

Specialized units, forget about it. The majority are white Irish and Italian who have these positions and will continue to have these positions. We presently have two lieutenants as commanders of squads within the detective bureau. There are no female blacks who command a squad. There are four females—I am one and believe me they just eliminated me—and six blacks male who are second whips or second in charge in a detective bureau.

Former Police Commissioners Patrick Murphy and Benjamin Ward were the only commissioners who addressed this disparity of detectives in grade designations. Due to the lack of significant numbers throughout the ranks for over a 20-year period, there have been an average of four African-American captains on promotion list at one time.

For the first time in the history of the New York City Police Department, we have an African-American female captain who was not recognized at the promotional ceremonies by our Police Commissioner Bratton as being the first African-American female captain, but recognized the fact that we have our first female chief in the history of our department, who is white.

Evaluations is another area in which we fall by the wayside. The evaluation is supposed to reflect the job the officer does.

Many times the officers are evaluated on other than their performance duties. African-Americans are evaluated on personality, color of their skin, whether they are light or dark skinned, and how well they can discipline other African-Americans.

Even though this process was recently reviewed and changed, we, the Guardians Association, feel that they are still too general and too biased. African-Americans are requesting other assignments to specialized units. They are often judged by these evaluations and often they do not even get a chance to see their evaluations.

Clearly, I am in that situation right now. During the 12 years that I have been on the job I have always had above standards and well above standards throughout this job. Since I've been President of the Guardians Association, I now meet standards with this department. I have had two evaluations during the last year.

I was on temporary assignment to recruitment for 10 months. My supervisor rated me well above standards. When I got back to my unit, which is Special Investigations Division, Missing Persons Squad, my lieutenant, Lieutenant Davis, had to rate me for two months out of that year.

He gave me "meets standards." He did not look at the well above standards that my prior boss gave me, who is a deputy chief. He didn't even take it into consideration. He felt that since I was not there for 10 months out of the year, I was not a team player and I did not deserve to get an above standards, even a well above standards.

Because of the color of my skin and because I speak out for what I believe in, I got "meets standards." The evaluation reads "meets department requisite standings." I don't know what that is. He could not explain that to me.

One of my white Italian counterparts received a well above standards, and he was on terminal leave for eight months out of the same year. He came back because he has a lawsuit in court for age discrimination because he is 64 years old. Until he wins his suit, he is given well above standards.

He does not have a team. He does not do evaluations. He is not there, but is still being given well above standards.

Former Chief of Department Robert Johnston, who is white, was one of the few chiefs who addressed the disparity in assignments of the police department. He took it upon himself to assign African-Americans to positions where they were previously excluded.

We have no African-Americans in the Harbor Unit. We have two in aviation. We have no bureau chiefs in the Bureau of Detectives that are African-American.

We had one, Chief Benjamin Foster, but Brooklyn North, the black unit, needed a chief so they transferred him to Brooklyn North back to patrol. That left a spot for Chief of Detectives and a white Irish Chief Hill could get that position; he will have that position in another two months.

Ms. WHITE-RUIZ. He has it.

Ms. RIDLEY. Excuse me; he has it.

Within the Patrolman's Benevolent Police Association there are no African-Americans on the board of trustees. In order to get elected to the board, you must win votes in all ethnic groups and then some. With only 11 percent African-Americans in the New York City Police Department—this includes detectives, sergeant, lieutenants, captains and above who cannot vote in this election—all the African-Americans could not overcome the votes to get on this board.

The Patrolman's Benevolent Association has no African-American attorneys in its law firm and our less than 11 percent needs some African-American representation at times and they request it, but PBA denies hiring to African-Americans.

To date, PBA has discriminated against African-American officers with unfair representation at hearings, trials in both department and city courts. They have continued to use our officers' funds without permission to run ad campaigns in newspapers, radio, and TV; to make donations to white colleges; and they have investments in South Africa.

It is clear that PBA does not have our best interests at heart.

Chairman OWENS. Are you required to join the PBA?

Ms. RIDLEY. Mandated. As soon as you put your hand up, they have your money. You have to be part of the PBA because they are a negotiating union.

Mr. SANDERS. Unless they kick you out.

Chairman OWENS. That is what I wanted the record to show.

Ms. RIDLEY. We are making a recommendation that through these hearings, it may be possible to have Guardians Association have its own dues checkoff system.

Corruption comes in all forms in the New York City Police Department. The commissioner states that he is hard on drugs and shakedowns and free meals; yet he cannot control the inner departmental corruption that happens every day in this department. There are deals made all the time and most of them do not include African-Americans.

Commissioner Bratton has also stated that "There are no qualified African-Americans to fill top positions within the New York City Police Department," and we, the City of New York would not see a great number of African-Americans within the New York City Police Department until the next century.

The demographics of the New York City Police Department have not changed in the last 20 years and they are slowly diminishing every year.

We recommend that the commission set up standards for evaluations pass-fail criteria and take it away from the Department of Personnel because they do not have our best interests at heart. Had it not been for the employment of African-American women, lawsuits for entrance examinations, lawsuits for the promotion to captain, lieutenant and sergeant by the Guardians Association, recruitment of the Guardians Association, the retention program by the Guardians Association and the tutorial programs, the census of African-Americans within the New York City Police Department would have greatly diminished years ago.

We are also part of the Federation of the African-American Civil Service Workers. They are appalled because there are so many of them—I am talking about State parole, State courts, housing authority, and hospitals, taxi and limousine—there are so many.

I must state for the record if we plan to correct the discriminatory practice in law enforcement agencies, we must not use the same practices hereby allowing other people to testify, not that I have a problem with it, but I do because we could have brought—I have Rod Gideons here to testify as a retired police officer from my organization and a member of the federation.

I had my President from the Transit Association who was a little angry and left because he did not receive an invitation.

Currently there is no affirmative action program in place for the New York City Police Department. The only affirmative action adhered to is by direction of the courts as a result of Guardians Association lawsuits.

At this time, I would like to let you know that we have requested from our Records Office in the New York City Police Department, under the Freedom of Information law, the candidates disqualified during applicant processing, the OEO breakdown, the CCRB complaints, evaluations and classifications, command disciplines filed and dispositions in our trial rooms, which is another kangaroo court, charges and specifications which are filed and dispositions because we don't have a clue of how many African-Americans get caught up in that system.

We are falling by the wayside on these practices by the New York City Police Department. There are many articles out there. It goes on because they don't play by the rules. Until there are guidelines set up, we won't get ahead.

If this panel and these hearings are just for political reasons, then I am appalled. If we are going to do something, we need to do it now, because it is too late for us to correct the wrongs when we have brothers and sisters laid off and cannot get this job.

We need to look to the future. We have 270 candidates in the academy now and they are dropping like flies because of discriminatory practices.

My son is in the academy now and he was told that he had to pick up soap gratings from a shower because he was on limited duties, and that was supposed to be in his job description. When he told the instructor that it wasn't in his job description and that he wouldn't have told his white counterparts to do that, he was told they were going to bring him up on charges and specifications.

New York inspectors are not custodians. My son didn't tolerate it. We are going to go the whole road with this if we have to take them to court and sue them for everything they got.

I thank you.

[The prepared statement of Ms. Ridley follows:]

84-118 - 94 - 3

Good Morning. I am Grace E. Ridley, President of the Guardians Association, New York City Police Department Inc. I would like to thank the members of the Committee on Education and Labor, Subcommittee on select Education and Civil Rights for the opportunity to address this body regarding discrimination practices in promotions, evaluations and inner department corruption within the New York City Police Department.

Due to the short notice with receiving my invitation to testify at this hearing, I am shocked and dismayed to think that in two (2) days of notification, I could give you an accurate number of cases documented of blatant discriminatory practices and racism within the New York City Police Department.

Issues

1. Residency - ALL persons hired by the New York City Police Department for position of Police Officer should be New York City residents. We feel that persons living within the New York City area, would be better suited for Police Officers. They have a vested interest in the city in which they live (ie: family, pay taxes); would be more responsible to the well being of others in heart, but above all the department be more representative of the citizens of the City of New York.

2. Discriminatory practices in hiring - There are currently four (4) existing lists of candidates. (#9006, 0079,* 1007 and * 1177 - *Two of which have yet to be promulgated. Test #9006 will expire 10/94, Test #0079 will expire 03/95 and Test #0294 will expire 07/95.

The investigative process in the Applicant Processing Division should be challenged, and needs to be revamped. There should be more African American medical doctors and psychologists employed by the New York City Police Department. This would possibly ensure that fair and unbiased practices would be implemented. Although, there are only two African Americans who head the Medical and Psychological Units (they have contact with candidates entering the department on a limited basis), there are no African American psychologists who conduct interviews and test in-coming candidates, nor are there medical doctors or nurses who conduct medical examinations for candidates/cadets entering this department.

The African American candidates are often discriminated against before they ever begin the investigation process with their investigators. They are disqualified as soon as they walk through the door by their case investigators (who are 90% white have a biased opinion about African Americans from their upbringing, have limited contact with other ethnic groups and tend to bring these prejudices with them to the agency.

African American candidates are usually disqualified for:
1) Not being employed for 2-3 years 2) having babies out of wedlock 3) Appeal process

(These practices are deemed to be discriminatory for African Americans, but valid reasons for white candidates). As a police officer you can acquire information from your investigator as to your position (past or fail) on the psychological from your investigator. In order to appeal a failure, the written confirmation is received from the department on an average of nine (9) months later. The timing almost excludes you from appealing because this process takes almost an additional year. The Department of Personnel have abdicated their responsibility in reference to the psychological appeals and in essence the Police Department is appealing itself.

At least 50% of the candidates have taken 2-3 examinations and could possibly be on two or three lists awaiting to be hired. A true number of persons awaiting to be hired is not available at this time. The reason the candidates are on different lists, is to have some type of insurance that will give them a second chance to be employed in case the list dies, their investigation is held over, medical or psychological or character investigations are being reviewed. (Appeals process stated in previous paragraph). Investigators often carry approximately 150-200 cases . The possibly exists that case investigators will select "cream puff" cases (easiest cases possible with the least work involved), to pass through processing. These cases are not those of African Americans candidates. The unit is understaffed and investigators handled too many cases. The New York City Police Department Cadet Program is approximately 85% African Americans. They are usually screened out with the same bias practices in the medical and psychological and character investigations even though they are initially qualified upon becoming a cadet.

In addition, the investigation process is often an excruciating experience for African Americans. They are humiliated, disrespected, and on numerous occasions, told, "they are wasting their time". This results in many African Americans dropping out of the process. The Department lacks adequate retention procedures which is crucial to the African American candidates.

As per prior testimony at the Equal Employment Practices commission March, 1993 states:

" AFRICAN AMERICAN CANDIDATES ARE NOT AS SUCCESSFUL AS MAJORITY CANDIDATES ON THE CHARACTER INVESTIGATIONS AND PSYCHOLOGICAL SCREENING. AFRICAN AMERICAN CANDIDATES ALSO APPEAR TO DISCONTINUE PROCESSING AT A HIGHER RATE THAN MAJORITY CANDIDATES. THE COMBINES EFFECT RESULTS IN AN AFRICAN AMERICAN APPOINTMENT RATE WHICH IS LESS THAN THAT WHICH IS HOPED FOR."

Historical Perspective

A 1971 study by the New York City Rand Institute entitled "Minority Recruiting in the New York City Police Department," discussed issues relating to the attraction and retention of minority candidates. According to the study, one major factor accounting for under-representation of minority group members is the high rate of attrition among applicants who passed the exam but withdrew from the hiring process. The study noted that this dropout rate was higher among African Americans that other ethnic groups.

The limited employment of African Americans as pokice officers by the New York City Police Department has been the subject of analysis for more than twenty years. Studies of this issue have focused on racial bias within the New York City Police Department and discriminatory hiring procedures. Gains in hiring made by African Americans have been attributed in large to legal challenges to the discriminatory employment practices if the New York City Police Department. In 1979, (exam #8155) the Guardians Association (as association of African American police officers) sued the City, charging that the police examination was discriminatory. The Court found that the examination had a disparate impact on minorities. As a result, the City was directed to achieve a minority hiring ratio of 33% pending development of valid selection procedures. Again, we find ourselves in the same situation of fighting discriminatory practices, (both Captain's and Lieutenant's examinations) and both a compromised and disparate impact of African Americans on Sergeants examination (New York City Sergeant Examination #1528).

There were allegations of wide-spread cheating on Sergeants Examination and a alleged arrest made, but Commissioner William Bratton continues to promote off a list of approximately 3000, where ONLY approximately 50 African Americans are identified.

When this allegation of cheating first came to the Guardians Association's attention, (November, 1993), we notified Mayor Dinkins, Mayor elect Guilliani, Commissioner Raymond Kelly, New York City Police Department, Herman Jenkins, City Personnel Director, Department of Personnel, Department Of Investigations, and Internal Affairs Bureau, New York City Police Department. The allegation included a Police Administrative Aide who alleged to have removed the test from a test site on the Sabbath Observers day of examination (Prior to 10/26/93). We have not heard any information relative to that allegation, but shortly thereafter the New York City Police Department started to make Provisional Sergeants (approximately 600 from the existing list - ONLY 10 were African Americans).

Approximately five months to date, on April 21, 1994, Housing Police Officer Robert Temple was arrested on charges of Criminal Possession of Stolen Property 4th Degree and other related charges. The officer was allegedly in possession of the Sergeant examination #1528 which substantiates our allegations of possible compromising of this examination.

3. Promotions

Within the New York City Police Department, there are three (3) grades in the Detective Rank. There are monetary increases:

Third Grade - salary from Police officer to Sergeant
Second Grade- Equivalent to Sergeant's salary
First Grade - Equivalent to Lieutenant's salary

We have African Americans who presently have a minimum of twenty (20) years of service with the New York City Police Department and have sixteen (16) years as a Third Grade Detective.

The New York City Police Department has recently set up a criteria for grade assignment within the last two years, but has not devised a plan to include African Americans to be promoted prior to this criteria. So Detectives 3rd grade assignment (mostly African Americans) have no way to reach to standards of the 90's and all their work from sixteen years ago, go unrewarded. The white officers who have relatives on the job as Chiefs, Inspectors, etc., will get put on a grid (data base system) and you can not tell where you stand as far as promotion goes. These promotions are based by panel decision, and you are not told of results upon completion of the interview process.

Former Police Commissioners Patrick Murphy and Benjamin Ward were the ONLY commissioners to address this disparity of Detective Grade designations.

Due to the lack of significant numbers throughout the ranks, for over a twenty (20) year period, there have only been an average of four (4) African Americans on the Captains Promotional lists at one time. For the first time in the history of the New York City Police Department, we have a African American Female Captain, who was not recognized at the promotion ceremony by our Police Commissioner as being the FIRST AFRICAN AMERICAN FEMALE CAPTAIN, but recognized the first female Chief in the history of the department.

4. Evaluations

When evaluating Police Officers within the New York City Police Department, the evaluations are to be reflective of the job the officer does. Many times, the Officers are evaluated on other then their performance of duties. African Americans are evaluated on how personality, color of their skin (light or dark), how well they can discipline other African Americans, etc. Even though this procedure was recently reviewed and changed, we (Guardians Association) feel that it is still too general and biased. When African Americans are requesting other assignments to specialized units, they are often judged by the evaluations, which often time the officer does not even see how the rater has evaluated him/her.

Former Chief of Department Robert Johnston, who is white, was one of the few Chiefs who addressed the disparity assignments in the New York City Police Department. He took it upon himself to assign African Americans to positions they were previously excluded from.

5. Patrolman's Benevolent Association, New York City Police Department

There are no African Americans on the Board Of trustees in this organization. In order for you to get elected on the board, you must win votes from ALL OTHER ETHNIC GROUPS and then some. With only 11% African Americans in the New York City Police Department (11% total includes Detectives, Sergeants, Lieutenants, Captains and above who cannot vote with this union) all the African Americans could not overcome enough votes to get on the Board.

The Patrolman's Benevolent Association has no African American attorneys with its Law firm to represent African American officers.

To date, the P.B.A. has discriminated against African American officers with unfair representation at hearings, trials (both department and City Courts). They have continuously used our officers funds without permission to run ad campaigns in the newspapers, radio and on television, made donations to white colleges, and have made investments in South Africa. It is clear that the P.B.A. does not have our best interest at heart. (News Clipings)

6. Corruption

Corruption comes in all forms in the New York City Police Department. The Commissioner states he's hard on Drugs, Shake-downs, free meals, free coffee, etc. Yet, he cannot control in inner department corruption that happens every day in the department. There are deals made all the time, and most of them DO NOT include African Americans.

Commissioner Bratton has stated "There were no qualified African Americans to fill top positions within the New York City Police Department", and we (the City of New York) would not see a great number of African Americans within the New York City Police Department until the next century".

The demographics in the New York City Police Department have not change in the last twenty (20) years and they are slowly diminishing each and every year.

Conclusion:

Had it not been for the employment of African American women, lawsuits for entrance examinations, lawsuits for promotion to Captain, Lieutenant, Sergeants by this the Guardians Association; the Recruitment, Guardians Association retention Program, and the Guardians Association Tutorial Programs, the census of the African Americans within the New York City Police Department would have greatly diminished years ago.

There is presently no Affirmative Action Program in place in the New York City Police Department. The ONLY Affirmative Action adheres to is by the direction from the Courts, via Guardians Association lawsuits.

Thank you for the opportunity address this body and present testimony on discriminatory practices within the New York City Police Department.

Monday, June 13, 1994

Guardians Association of the Police Department

OF THE CITY OF NEW YORK INC.

P.O. BOX 87, PECK SLIP STATION, NEW YORK, N.Y. 10272-0087

FOR IMMEDIATE RELEASE

Contact: Grace E. Ridley, President
Phone: 917-616-6224 Pager #
Contact: Eric Sanders, 1st Vice President
Phone: 917-253-6171 Pager #

Promotion to Sergeant, New York City Police Department
Examination # 1528

New York, N.Y., June 13,1994

On November 22, 1993, the Guardians Association requested an investigation be commenced by an independent authority. Regarding, several allegations brought to this association's attention, of possible comprising of Promotion to Sergeant, New York City Police Department, Examination # 1528.
(See enclosed correspondence)

Since our original allegations, Former Police Commissioner Kelly's Office received several anonymous letters alleging possible wrongdoing. The allegations were consolidated and classified as "Unsubstantiated."

On December 16, 1993, the Guardians Association received correspondence from Former City Personnel Director, Herbert L. Jenkins Department of Personnel. Basically, acknowledging receipt of our request, referring the case to the Department of Investigation and requesting this association to reserve comment, until the investigation is complete.
(See enclosed correspondence)

Approximately five months to date, on April 21, 1994, Housing Police Officer Robert Temple was arrested on charges of Criminal Possession of Stolen Property 4 and several other charges. The officer was allegedly in possession of Promotion to Sergeant, New York City Police Department, Examination # 1528. This arrest substantiates our allegations of possible compromising of this examination.
(See enclosed newspaper article)

Guardians Association
OF THE POLICE DEPARTMENT
CITY OF NEW YORK

In 1991, the Transit Police Department was rocked by similar allegations involving Promotion to Sergeant, New York City Transit Police Department Examination # 0539. The investigation was initiated by an anonymous letter to the Transit Police Department's, Internal Affairs Unit. The letter outlined allegations against an African-American Lieutenant, who allegedly was part of an informal study group at his home. He reportedly directed perspective candidates to areas in a preparatory instruction manual and where to concentrate their study. The examination was invalidated on September 13, 1991. The Lieutenant was subsequently convicted of Official Misconduct and other related charges. He is expected to receive a sentence including incarceration.
(See enclosed newspaper article)

We expect the Department of Personnel to acknowledge the breach of security and abrogate the current eligible list. Furthermore, the Department of Personnel should seek consultation with a private consulting firm and vendor to assemble the next promotional examination. This task should be undertaken with minimal Police Department involvement. The next examination should be administered within two years.

We expect parallel investigations to be conducted by the State Civil Service Commission, Manhattan District Attorney's, Integrity Bureau, Department of Investigation, Deputy Commissioner of Internal Affairs, Special Investigative Unit and the New York City Housing Police Department's, Internal Affairs Bureau.

We would like to offer the following recommendations:

1. Administer a different examination to the Sabbath Observer
2. The investigators' should explore the idea of turning the arrested officer in hopes of discovering the breach of security
3. The investigators' should also assess the role if any, promotional schools such as: K.S.A., played in this breach of security.

We expect the investigating agencies to pursue any and all leads aggressively, in hopes of bringing forth a successful criminal prosecution, of all violators of applicable State and City Statutes.

The Guardians Association, is an African-American fraternal organization in the New York City Police Department. We received a Charter to operate on July 6, 1949. The organization was formed to lead the struggle against disparate treatment towards African-Americans. Our membership is mainly composed of active and retired members of the New York City Police Department. The association represents well over 8000 members.

Guardians Association of the Police Department

OF THE CITY OF NEW YORK INC.

504 MARION STREET, BROOKLYN, N.Y. 11233

November 22, 1993

Mr. Herman Jenkins
Director, New York City Department of Personnel
2 Washington Street
New York, New York 10004

Re: **POSSIBLE COMPROMISE OF THE 1993 N.Y.C.P.D. SERGEANT'S EXAMINATION #1528**

Dear Mr. Jenkins,

It has come to the attention of our organization that the 1993 Sergeant's Promotional Examination (1528) may have been compromised. The Guardians Association is gravely concerned about the following and request that an investigation be commenced by an independent authority:

The following has been brought to our attention:

1. That a copy of the examination was removed from a test site (Sabbath Observers Exam) and was distributed to members taking the test prior to October 26, 1993.

2) At least one testing location, officers were allowed to use their Patrol Guide for the entire examination.

3) There is a question as to the allocation of test sites, it appears that the majority of minority officers were assigned to one location bypassing other sites which were closer to their residence.

It is requested that if any or all of the above allegations are true that a serious consideration be given to the scheduling of a new exam. We are aware of the high cost to the city, yet the need to preserved the integrity of the exam process can not be over stated. Since the action of compromising a civil service exam is a violation of law, we expect that the violators will be dealt with in accordance with law.

Sincerely,

Robert Rivers Jr.
President

DEPARTMENT OF
PERSONNEL
OF THE CITY OF NEW YORK

2 WASHINGTON STREET, NEW YORK, NY 10004

HERMAN L. JENKINS
CITY PERSONNEL DIRECTOR

December 16, 1993

Mr. Robert Rivers Jr.
President
Guardians Association of the
Police Department
504 Marion Street,
Brooklyn, NY 11233

Dear Mr. Rivers:

This letter is in response to your concerns regarding the allegations that the examination for Promotion to Sergeant, NYCPD, Examination No. 1528 may have been compromised.

We are aware of the allegations surrounding the administration of the above examination. The Department of Investigations (DOI) is currently investigating this matter. While we recognize the severity of the situation, it would be imprudent to respond to the allegations before DOI has completed their investigation.

Sincerely,

Herman L. Jenkins

HLJ:gm

CHIEF LEADER APRIL 1, 1994

On Sergeant Promo

Lieut. Convicted Of Revealing Test Info

A Transit Police Lieutenant with 12 years on the force faces possible jail time and dismissal for revealing information about a 1991 examination for Sergeant that was later invalidated by the city Personnel Department. More than 1,800 Transit Police Officers took the test.

The Lieutenant, Michael Gordon, has been convicted of supplying information related to Exam 0539 to three officers. The officers, two of whom are to stand trial on charges of lying about the help they received from Lieutenant Gordon, were part of an informal study group that Mr. Gordon led in his home, according to a spokesman for the Manhattan District Attorney's Office, which handled the prosecution.

Sentencing May 13

Lieutenant Gordon is scheduled to be sentenced on May 13 in Manhattan Supreme Court.

Mr. Gordon wrote and reviewed questions that appeared on the Feb. 2, 1991 exam. According to the DA's Office, he directed the three officers to areas in a preparatory instruction manual from which questions were derived. "He told those prospective test-takers where to concentrate their study," the spokesman, Gerald McKelvey, said.

"There was no testimony that he did this in exchange for money or anything of value," Mr. McKelvey said. "It appears he did it out of friendship."

The Personnel Department invalidated the exam on Sept. 13, 1991 following a Department of Investigation finding that the test had been "compromised."

The Transit Police Department's Internal Affairs Unit had learned of allegations about Lieutenant Gordon's disclosure from an anonymous letter, according to a Transit P.D. spokesman.

Guardians Were Critical

The Transit Police Guardians Association, a black fraternal group, had disputed the determination the exam was compromised and criticized its invalidation, saying it was a disservice to many black officers who had fared well. According to the Personnel Department, 68 of 317 black officers, or 21 percent, passed the exam, compared with 76 of 550 blacks, or 14 percent, on the prior promotional in 1987.

There had been rumors within the department that black officers had received advance information on the exam. Lieutenant Gordon and the three officers he was convicted of helping are black.

Mr. McKelvey said the DA's Office had no information that the three officers shared what they learned from Lieutenant Gordon with other officers. He noted that the Guardians Association had assisted in the investigation.

The Transit P.D. also had no evidence that more officers obtained an unfair advantage, despite the rumors, according to the depart-

(Continued on Page 6)

Lieutenant Is Convicted

(Continued from Page 1)

ment's spokesman, Albert W. O'Leary.

Initially, the Manhattan DA's Office found that it lacked evidence to gain an indictment. However, new evidence was developed, according to Mr. McKelvey, and Mr. Gordon was indicted on March 2, 1992. He was convicted March 11 on charges of official misconduct and obstructing civil service rights after a jury trial.

The crimes for which he was found guilty are misdemeanors, which each carry a jail term of up to one year.

Faces Dismissal

Lieutenant Gordon has been placed on "modified duty" pending the outcome of administrative charges that could lead to his being fired, Mr. O'Leary said.

Officers Samuel James and David Tarquini are charged with perjury for allegedly telling the grand jury that handed up the indictment of Lieutenant Gordon that they did not attend meetings in Mr. Gordon's home when he made information about Exam 0539 available.

The jury in Lieutenant Gordon's trial found that Officers Tarquini and James were two of the test-takers whom Mr. Gordon briefed prior to the exam. Lieutenant Gordon briefed a third individual, whose name was not revealed and who is not being charged, according to the DA's Office.

A.D.M.

Corruption Net Must Catch Police Brass

SYDNEY H. SCHANBERG

FORMER POLICE Commissioner Raymond Kelly phoned me last Friday to protest that I had maligned him in my column on police corruption that day.

I had written that the only cops arrested and held accountable in the latest corruption scandal, in the 30th Precinct, were patrol officers at the bottom of the ladder, while no action was taken against supervisors, including many of the top brass, who had early knowledge of the corruption and had done nothing about it. (This has been the pattern in every such scandal in modern New York City history).

Kelly was first deputy commissioner from 1990 to 1992, and in my column I included him in the group with early knowledge. I still do.

Kelly, in our phone conversation, said he never saw any corruption reports on the 30th Precinct in that period or had any conversation with any of his colleagues about that corruption or indeed had heard anything at all about it. He focused on one particular passage in the column, which read:

"On the chain of command, [Chief Robert] Beatty [then head of Internal Affairs, the unit that is supposed to police the police department] was required to pass corruption reports upward to Chief Daniel Sullivan, head of Inspectional Services, who in turn had to pass them up to First Deputy Commissioner Raymond Kelly. Thus all these men, and perhaps Commissioner Lee Brown as well, had to know that the 30th was a swamp of corruption."

Kelly said this was false as it pertained to him, because in the paper-routing organizational chart set up by Commissioner Brown, corruption reports were not "required" to go to Kelly as first deputy commissioner. Kelly said that when Sullivan got them from Beatty in Internal Affairs, he sent them not to Kelly but directly to Brown. Kelly insisted he was not a "close friend" of Beatty, as I had written, and knew him "only in a professional way."

Kelly was known throughout Brown's tenure as the de facto man in charge, a hands-on commander.

"In no way," he said, "was I in the chain of command then on Internal Affairs." He said the job of first deputy commissioner was "strictly an administrative post," making it sound as if he were some kind of off-to-the-side personnel manager with narrow duties.

I choose to accept without quibble that Kelly is right and I was wrong about the paper-routing requirement. That gives him technical deniability.

But the information I received from strong, inside sources, some of them unknown to the others and providing separate confirmation, says that Kelly was one of those with early knowledge, whether or not he ever saw a particular piece of paper.

Kelly was known throughout Brown's tenure as the de facto man in charge, a hands-on commander. Brown was not only more insulated from daily operations but out of his office and out of town on a regular basis. Kelly was in de jure charge on those occasions. Highly placed insiders frankly scoff at his contention that he was out of the loop, saying he couldn't have been — he ran the loop.

For example, when Kelly was in command during Brown's absences, what happened to the paper reports from Internal Affairs then — the ones that he said were routed to Brown?

Once before, Kelly raised eyebrows by claiming he was out of the loop. He said he learned about the Crown Heights riots in August, 1991, only when he turned on the television news at home. Kelly had formerly commanded the Crown Heights precinct.

But this isn't about a dispute between a reporter and a former police official. Nor is it about Ray Kelly personally, who was mentioned in the column not as a leading culprit, but merely in a list of names of police brass to demonstrate the behavioral pattern of people at the top when corruption surfaces — a pattern of sweeping it under the rug.

If Ray Kelly or any of the others who say they knew nothing were really completely in the dark, then wasn't this an enormous departmental failure and shouldn't the brass therefore accept responsibility for it?

I asked Ray Kelly this question. I also asked him why, in such instances, the brass didn't at least get demoted and have to retire on reduced pensions. He did not respond directly. But his overall response to the column was: "You want heads to roll. It makes for good writing. You love this conspiracy theory."

William Bratton, the commissioner who replaced Kelly this year, has taken a tough public stance against police corruption, staging the arrests in the 30th Precinct so that the accused patrol officers would be led out of the stationhouse in handcuffs before television cameras. He says that if they're convicted, he'll retire their badges in some kind of museum of shame.

Yet while preparing the gallows for these street cops, he has set forth a quite different standard for their supervisors and presumably for the higher brass as well. He has tried to sell a bizarre notion to the press — that the supervisors, in particular the sergeants, didn't notice anything wrong because they were so overwhelmed with paperwork.

"That's crap," said a highly regarded retired officer. "You live in close quarters in a precinct. There are damned few secrets. If a supervisor has been there for a month and still says he doesn't know anything is going on, then he should at least be bounced back to patrol officer. That kind of denial borders on criminal behavior. And you can apply that right up the line to the top brass."

The majority of street cops happen to be honest, and there's no way you can restore pride and trust to a battered department if they're the only ones held to account.

GRAPHIC OPINION

Auth, The Philadelphia Inquirer

New York Newsday
Founded in 1940 by Alicia Patterson and Harry F. Guggenheim
Robert M. Johnson, Publisher & C.E.O.
Steven L. Isenberg, Deputy Publisher
Executive V.P. Operations: Alberto Ibargüen
Editor and Executive V.P.: Anthony Marro
TIMES MIRROR COMPANY: Robert F. Erburu, Chairman & President; David Laventhol, Editor-at-Large
SENIOR VICE PRESIDENTS: Special Projects: James E. Fitzgerald; Finance: Gerald H.L. Trybaux; Distribution: Harold F. Walsh Jr
VICE PRESIDENTS: Public Affairs and Assistant to the Publisher: Chiara Coletti; Human Resources: Elizabeth V. Drewry; New York Editor: Donald Forst; Information Systems: Thomas Reddin
EDITORIAL: Managing Editors: James Toedtman, Robert F. Brandt, Howard Schneider; Editorial Design Director: Robert Eisner; Photography Director: James C. Dooley; Associate Editor: Sydney H. Schanberg; Assistant Managing Editors: Richard Galant, Charlotte H. Hall, David C. Hamilton, Robert E. Keane, Les Payne, Steve Ruinsky, Phyllis Singer, Debra Whitefield
ADVERTISING: Director: John C. McKeon; Manager, N.Y. Retail: Carey Gates; Manager, L.I. Retail and Sales Administration: Patricia A. Burnagiel; Manager, National Major Accounts: Raymond J. McCutcheon; Manager, Classified: Bruce Murray; Manager, Direct Marketing: Thomas F. Reilly Jr
OPERATIONS: Director: Ed Hughes; Management Director: John P. Wills; Manager: Ken Sewald
HUMAN RESOURCES: Development Director: Richard Greene; Systems & Benefits Director: David A. Smukler
LABOR: Director: Carol H. Green
CIRCULATION: Transportation Director: Martin J. Bartow; N.Y. Manager: Robert Brennan; L.I. Manager: Fred Balbor
MARKETING SERVICES: Marketing Director: Randolph R. Charles; Promotion Director: Susan Fleischer; Research Manager: Edward P. Farrell
ADMINISTRATIVE SERVICES: Director: Frank E. Toner
PUBLIC AFFAIRS: N.Y. Manager: Diane McNulty; L.I. Manager: Peg Mancuso; Community and Employee Relations Director: Reginald Tuggle
FINANCE: Director: Nancy J. Ilo

APRIL 26, 1994 DAILY NEWS

Former finest want cops both blue and true

Somewhere near the heart of the NYPD's crisis of corruption and morale lies a simple truth: Ultimately, loyalty to your partner comes second to loyalty to the mission that bonded you in the first place: to protect the city, its neighborhoods and its children.

Only when that stops meaning anything does the "blue wall of silence" become truly impenetrable. The problem of corruption isn't just that cops are reluctant to snitch on other cops. It's that, for some, there's no sense of mission stronger than the admirable reluctance to snitch.

The meaning of being a cop has become overgrown by a cover-your-butt mentality that turns the system of incentives and punishments taught in the Police Academy upside down. That demoralizes good cops and sets the stage for corruption itself. Here's an example of the problem and some news about NYPD alumni who are going to do something about it.

A cop recently wrote me of a day years ago when, as an idealistic rookie, he arrived at his precinct to find a veteran officer in "silver bracelets." The Internal Affairs Division had caught the man dealing drugs while on duty, and he looked stunned and ashamed. But to the rookie's surprise, that wasn't how some of his fellow officers looked.

"We rookies were told, 'If you don't contribute to the defense fund for him, we'll put your name up on the bulletin board.' To most people in the command, the IAD cops were rats and scum. . . . They couldn't admit that IAD did its job and that the arrested cop was scum."

There, in a nutshell, is the problem. The "blue wall" isn't a wall. It's an active, high-pressure front that engulfs and devours any cop who tries to live by the rules.

Long before a cop even thinks of stealing or dealing, he or she learns that "the job isn't on the level." Assignments and promotions are decided on the basis of whom you know, what favors you've done

The strongest sense of 'mission' is a reluctance to snitch.

and — as your web of mutual debts expands — whether you can be counted on to look the other way. The spectacle of cops raising money for an officer who was caught red-handed disgracing them is a symptom, not the disease.

Call the disease Dominick Corso Syndrome, after a City Councilman who said years ago, "You think it takes guts to stand up for what is right? That doesn't take guts. What takes guts is to stand up for what you know is wrong, day after day."

Sure, rules are made to be broken. Good commanders apply the Patrol Guide flexibly to motivate officers. Demoralization sets in only when leaders use rules capriciously, to punish officers for reasons having nothing to do with performance and everything to do with internal politics.

Enter the Concerned Alliance for Professional Policing. It's a group of ex-NYPD investigators, supervisors and middle managers. Most were Police Academy instructors. Most have graduate degrees. Now they're private-sector executives, managers or self-employed business people. In May they'll finalize CAPP's bylaws, elect a nine-member governing board and reach out to Police Commissioner William Bratton, who most of them think is off to a good start.

What will CAPP do? "We're not just here to cheer for alma mater," says a founder. "We want to help the department dig deeper into itself in terms of being on the level. We want to end the theater of the absurd where top brass and union leaders routinely get three-quarter tax-free disability pensions. Demoralization starts right there.

"We want to help cops outside Internal Affairs get involved in investigations. The approach to corruption has always been, 'It's not your job, leave it to us.' But precinct commanders and supervisors should be involved in investigations, especially the ones they initiate."

That would help breach the blue wall.

'WE ALSO WANT to increase public awareness of when the NYPD is rendered ineffective by politicians, district attorneys and others in the criminal justice system," the spokesman says. "A police commissioner can't just criticize a DA or a judge. We can."

CAPP also will support community policing and child-protection and youth-development programs.

These ex-cops, whom I've met twice, can't stop thinking and caring about the department they left behind. There could be no finer tribute to the sometimes-forgotten mission of New York's Finest. We'll be hearing more from them soon.

Lack of suffering makes '90s kids totally miserable

While chatting with a young audience on MTV, President Clinton was asked about the deep sense of "emptiness" that so many youths feel in their lives. The President responded with an upbeat pep talk. He meant well, but it will take more than pep talks and inspirational slogans to cure the widespread emotional blahs that allegedly afflict millions of young Americans. Because of the seriousness of this problem, I recently discussed it with Dr. I.M. Kookie, the world-renowned expert on lots of stuff:

Why do so many young people have a deep sense of emptiness in their lives?

"Because they don't suffer and feel miserable."

But they say that they do suffer and feel miserable because of the sense of emptiness.

"That is a bad diagnosis. The fact is, their sense of emptiness is brought on by a lack of misery and suffering. If they were genuinely miserable, they would not feel emptiness. There is nothing that cures a sense of emptiness like true misery and suffering."

Are you saying misery and suffering can be beneficial?

"Absolutely. Check out all the top saints and martyrs of history. You think they got to be saints and martyrs by playing Nintendo, slouching around a mall, listening to self-pity rock music and whining about emptiness? No, they got out there and really suffered. I'm talking heavy pain and agony. It's kind of like clearing the emotional sinuses. But most young people don't get their daily dosage, so

NEW YORK NEWSDAY, THURSDAY, MAY 19, 1994

Stolen Sergeant's Exam Raises Questions

By Susan Forrest and William K. Rashbaum
STAFF WRITERS

The Police Academy instructor arrested with a stolen copy of the Police Department sergeant's exam received the test and answers before it was given in October, possibly jeopardizing the validity of the test taken by about 15,000 cops, court papers show.

The Internal Affairs Bureau is investigating whether Robert Temple, 25, a housing police officer who served as a police science instructor at the Police Department academy, sold copies of the test to other cops.

"It is still being investigated whether the test was jeopardized," said Sgt. John Clifford, a police spokesman. "No decision has been made."

Temple's attorney, Mitch Garber, said his client denies selling the exam and alleged "gross improprieties" by Internal Affairs in its investigation, but refused to elaborate..

A felony complaint filed in criminal court alleges that a woman officer working undercover for IAB taped several conversations with Temple between February and April in which he told her that, while at the academy, he "received a stolen copy of [the NYPD Sergeants Promotional Examination] including the answers."

The complaint also alleges that Temple offered the undercover officer $900 to obtain a copy of the upcoming Housing Police sergeant's exam, and that he paid her $150 on April 14 as a "first installment."

In addition, Internal Affairs investigators also uncovered evidence Temple admitted on tape that in early 1994 he fired his gun at a squeegee man on the Bowery and missed, according to the complaint.

The undercover officer also told authorities Temple "conspired" with her to "terrorize" a former girlfriend by planning to send nude photographs and videos of her to her fiance, according to the complaint.

On April 21, cops raided Temple's home and seized the stolen NYPD sergeant's exam and nude photographs. Temple was arrested and suspended without pay that day. The complaint charges Temple with fourth-degree criminal possession of stolen property, a felony, and other charges.

Arrest Clouds Sergeant Test

(Continued from Page 1)

former girlfriend to the woman's fiance.

Meanwhile, the former Transit Lieutenant convicted of divulging information concerning the 1991 Transit Sergeant exam was sentenced to six months in jail and fined $1,000 in State Supreme Court May 13.

The Lieutenant, Michael Gordon, 32, was convicted on two counts of official misconduct and three counts of obstructing civil service rights after a jury found him guilty of supplying information relating to Exam 0539.

State Supreme Court Justice Joan C. Sudolnick ordered Mr. Gordon, who was recently fired by the Transit Police Department, to report to jail May 27. Each of the five charges on which he was convicted carry a maximum one year in jail.

The 12-year veteran was charged on March 2, 1992 after authorities received an anonymous tip alleging Mr. Gordon, a writer and reviewer of questions on the Sergeant test, had briefed three applicants on the exam.

Two of those men, Officers Samuel James and David Tarquini, now face perjury charges after telling a grand jury that they did not attend informal tutoring sessions at Mr. Gordon's home.

The city Personnel Department nullified the Transit Sergeant exam on Sept. 13, 1991 after discovering the test had been compromised.

05-27-94

Housing Cop Arrested

Was P.D. Sergeant Test Compromised?

By SETH KAUFMAN

Last fall's Police Sergeant exam could be jeopardized with the disclosure of the arrest last month of a Housing Police Officer found in possession of a copy of the promotion test and its answers.

That news followed the sentencing of a former Transit Police Lieutenant who compromised a Transit Police Sergeant exam.

Found Copy in Home

Housing Police Officer Robert Temple, 25, was arrested and suspended on April 21 after allegedly telling an undercover cop he had obtained the NYPD Sergeant exam and answers prior to the test date while working at the Police Academy. Acting on a warrant, police subsequently seized a copy of the exam from Mr. Temple's home.

The test, Exam 1528, was administered in October to 12,738 Police Officers. Investigators with the NYPD Bureau of Internal Affairs are trying to ascertain whether Mr. Temple sold or distributed his copy to test applicants.

The NYPD has appointed 285 new Sergeants based on the October exam. Whether those promotions—as well as the test results—are in jeopardy of being invalidated will depend on the current investigation.

"The few times we've invalidated a list, it's been based on the findings of other agencies like the Department of Investigation," said Personnel Department spokeswoman Denise Collins.

Ms. Collins added that the test in question, which cost an estimated half a million dollars to administer, was a "released" exam, which means candidates were allowed to take the test booklet after completing the exam.

Papers filed in Manhattan Criminal Court by District Attorney Robert M. Morgenthau's office indicate Mr. Temple had more than a casual interest in police exams. According to the papers, Mr. Temple allegedly offered $900 to the undercover officer in return for a copy of an upcoming Housing Police Sergeant exam and made a downpayment of $150 towards the purchase.

Mr. Temple, who worked as a police science instructor at the Police Academy, was booked on two felony counts relating to both exams, criminal possession of stolen property and conspiracy. The counts carry a maximum sentence of up to four years. He is currently out on $5,000 bail.

Faces Other Charges

Mr. Temple also faces a number of charges for unrelated crimes, including reckless endangerment and conspiracy.

The first charge stems from an alleged confrontation Mr. Temple had with a "squeegee man" during which he fired his gun; the second, according to court papers, involved a plan to send nude photos and videos of his

(Continued on Page 8)

CHIEF - LEADER
05-27-94

06-10-94
CHIEF-LEADER

To Continue Sgt. Promos

As investigators try to ascertain whether a Housing Police Officer jeopardized last fall's Police Sergeant exam, promotions based on the results of the test will continue to be made, an official in the NYPD Personnel Bureau said.

"Right now, we don't have any reason to believe the test was compromised," Inspector Thomas Baumann told THE CHIEF-LEADER.

Questions about the test, which was administered last October, arose after Housing Police Officer Robert Temple was arrested April 21 after allegedly telling an undercover cop he had obtained copies of the promotion test and its answers prior to the exam date. Police later seized a copy of the exam and answers from Mr. Temple's home.

S.K.

Chairman OWENS. We certainly appreciate the scope of your testimony and the additional information you have given us.

It is my understanding that the subcommittee staff has been in touch with you since May and you have given us some recommendations. Two people who testified, officers White-Ruiz and Sanders, were both suggested by you, I understand, as witnesses.

We certainly would welcome broadening the inquiry to include those other agencies and other people that you just mentioned.

As to whether or not this is a political hearing, yes it is political. Politics is what power is all about. We want to use political power to correct some of these outrageous practices that go on and on, not just in New York City but all over. But New York City is a place where you should have less of this, but it seems we have more of it here than we have in other places.

We would like to pursue this. This subcommittee has never held hearings where it did not move to get results. We have a record which would submit to that.

So we are serious. The political system is what you have to use to adjust these grievances. It has not been used until now.

The details are very important, and you have come up with the details. People can rant and rave about discrimination, but unless you wade into details and use the system against itself, you will never get results.

Our final witness is Officer Osvaldo Rodriguez. We will schedule future hearings for those who wanted to testify and didn't have a chance to be heard.

Officer Rodriguez.

STATEMENT OF OSVALDO RODRIGUEZ, HARBOR UNIT, NEW YORK POLICE DEPARTMENT

Mr. RODRIGUEZ. Good afternoon.

Before I begin my testimony, I would like to take this opportunity to thank Chairman Major Owens and members of the Subcommittee on Select Education and Civil Rights for granting me this opportunity to be before you today. I would also like to thank my attorney, Mr. Norman Siegel, for his support.

I was born in New York City and raised by a single parent in Spanish Harlem. While growing up in Spanish Harlem, I learned the most important lesson, that is survival. I survived racial discrimination and poverty. Now I am faced with a battle on a different front; namely, employment discrimination.

In January 1984, I entered the New York City Police Department Training Academy. Upon graduation, I was assigned to patrol in the 10th Precinct and later to the 90th Precinct where I worked as a K–9 handler. After five years of precinct patrol and over one hundred arrests, I applied for and was accepted to the New York City Police Department Harbor Unit.

I had been told by other police officers that being accepted into this elite unit would be very difficult to achieve, almost impossible, and it was. It was difficult because it was very political, more a question of who you knew and not what you knew.

The selection process for entering the Harbor Unit has had, as I have pointed out in my complaint, a dramatic effect on minorities. For example, there are no minority supervisors, Latino supervisors,

Asian supervisors, black supervisors or female supervisors in the Harbor Unit and only the bare minimum of minority police officers as required by law.

Joining the Harbor Unit was the turning point of my career, a turn for the worst. Until then, my reputation as a police officer was commendable. Sadly, I am here today to tell you publicly—first, discrimination is alive and well among police officers.

Second, filing a complaint with NYPD OEEO was a bigger mistake than joining this elite unit of discrimination.

Third, the NYPD OEO is, in my opinion, inept.

The complaint that I filed with the NYPD OEEO regarding the Harbor Unit was not resolved. In fact, I dropped the complaint because I lost confidence in their ability to address my issues. I came to the realization that this office was more in the business of fulfilling a legal requirement than helping you.

My reporting discrimination to NYPD OEEO worked against me, because for the first time in my career as a police officer, I received a poor evaluation while in the Harbor Unit. This was my consolation prize for filing a complaint with NYPD OEEO.

All I desired was to become a pilot of a police launch like everyone aspires to be in the Harbor Unit. The poor evaluation was written as a result of my having filed the complaint. I say this with conviction because there was prior knowledge of my intent to file a complaint with NYPD OEEO.

This is retaliation. This violates my civil rights under Section 704(a) of the Civil Rights Act of 1964. Once again, the NYPD OEEO was notified and did nothing to address this act of retaliation, although I was told by them that it would be investigated separate and apart from my original complaint.

To clarify my impetus for filing with OEO, I would like to read from my original complaint dated December 8, 1993, to Deputy Commissioner, Office of Equal Employment Opportunity from myself; Subject: Complaint of Employment Discrimination.

"I, Police Officer Osvaldo Rodriguez, Shield Number 22155, assigned to the New York City Police Department Harbor Unit, desire to exercise my right to file a complaint of employment discrimination in accordance with Patrol Guide Procedure 120–12.

"This complaint is based upon the overt actions, deliberate actions that have been preferred against me and that have prevented my progress in terms of opportunities, assignments, seniority, and qualifications.

"Harbor Unit: The Harbor Unit has only recently begun an affirmative action program designed to admit minorities. The Harbor Unit has been an exclusive entity allowing only select ethnic groups to enter. Prior to affirmative action, assignment to the Harbor Unit had more to do with nepotism, favoritism and political association. The Harbor Unit has been slow to reverse this inclination and to change with the times. As with any change, there is resistance. The resistance is on the part of the administration and police officers alike.

"Complaint: I had been permanently assigned to the Harbor Unit since April 2, 1990. What I have encountered since then has implications of a continuance towards preventing minorities from realizing their potential. This condition has not been explained or resolved. As a result, assignments have been unfair, preferential and have interfered with my seniority, advancement and qualification in favor of other police officers that are assigned to the Harbor Unit.

"My desire has been to be a pilot of a police launch. On July 2, 1993, I obtained a United States Coast Guard license as a master, inland of vessels up to 100 gross tons, mate, near coastal of vessels up to 100 gross tons.

To achieve this objective I purchased a $600 home study course offered by Houston Marine and spent approximately $180 in application fees to fulfill the Coast Guard licensing requirements. In addition, I spent six months of studious work preparing for this exam on my own time. Furthermore, I attended a one-week course offered by the Harbor Unit reviewing for this exam.

"Implications: My seniority has been placed in jeopardy. There are some police officers assigned to the Harbor Unit with less seniority, less time in the Harbor Unit, and with no U.S. Coast Guard license who have been designated as pilots.

" Conclusion: Although a United States Coast Guard license is not a requirement of the Harbor Unit, it is looked upon very favorably by the Commanding Officer, the Police Department, and the United States Coast Guard. The license distinguishes a police officer from all the others.

"For a member of the Harbor Unit, it represents a dedication to the Police Department's ideals regarding higher education. To possess this license demonstrates that an individual is prepared to assume additional responsibilities.

"On the subject of opportunity, I have not heard any reasonable explanation for my delay in becoming a pilot of a police launch, so I continue to wait. I believe four years is excessive, unreasonable, and requires an explanation. To date, no adverse comments about any deficiencies as to my work habits, seamanship, pilotage abilities, knowledge of the post, attitude or punctuality have been made to me by anyone.

"Therefore, I have no choice but to conclude that there is more to my situation than meets the eye. I refer this complaint to the Office of Equal Employment Opportunity for a resolution that is equitable and hopefully will change the outlook for future minority groups who desire to change the Harbor Unit."

That is what I submitted to NYPD OEEO.

I have submitted a request for a transfer out of the Harbor Unit. I desire to move on before I become a victim of a witch-hunt. I do not at this time recommend that minority police officers file a complaint with NYPD OEEO until Commissioner Bratton has had an opportunity to evaluate that office, recommend change and make it more responsive to its stated purpose.

Conversely, if any minority police officer desires an assignment with an elite unit, beware the pitfalls. To them, you may still only represent a quota. In spite of this, you should achieve what you desire because education is the key to opportunity. It is not the answer to the question of employment discrimination, but it is a formidable ally.

This episode, ladies and gentlemen, is only the beginning of my journey into the abyss. I am concerned because I have 9½ years to serve as a New York City police officer and I want to contribute in a positive way.

So I sit here before you today to ask for your help in resolving my seemingly difficult situation. Why? Because I will not tolerate discrimination in any form against anyone. I am a New York City police officer.

Thank you.

[The prepared statement of Mr. Rodriguez follows:]

DATE: JUNE 13, 1994

FROM: POLICE OFFICER OSVALDO RODRIGUEZ, NYPD

TO: COMMITTEE ON EDUCATION AND LABOR,
SUBCOMMITTEE FIELD HEARING ON DISCRIMINATION IN LAW ENFORCEMENT AGENCIES.

SUBJECT: NEW YORK CITY POLICE DEPARTMENT, HARBOR UNIT - OFFICE OF EQUAL EMPLOYMENT OPPORTUNITY, LOG #433/93

DISTINGUISHED MEMBERS OF THIS PANEL, LADIES AND GENTLEMEN MY NAME IS POLICE OFFICER OSVALDO RODRIGUEZ.

BEFORE I BEGIN MY TESTIMONY, I WOULD LIKE TO TAKE THIS OPPORTUNITY TO THANK CHAIRMAN MAJOR OWENS AND MEMBERS OF THE SUBCOMMITTEE ON SELECT EDUCATION AND CIVIL RIGHTS FOR GRANTING ME THIS OPPORTUNITY TO BE HERE BEFORE YOU TODAY. I WOULD ALSO LIKE TO THANK MY ATTORNEY, MR. NORMAN SIEGEL FOR HIS SUPPORT.

I WAS BORN IN NEW YORK CITY AND RAISED BY A SINGLE PARENT IN SPANISH HARLEM. WHILE GROWING UP IN SPANISH HARLEM I LEARNED A MOST IMPORTANT LESSON. THAT IS SURVIVAL. I SURVIVED RACIAL DISCRIMINATION AND POVERTY. NOW I AM FACED WITH A BATTLE ON A DIFFERENT FRONT. NAMELY, EMPLOYMENT DISCRIMINATION.

ON JANUARY 1984, I ENTERED THE NEW YORK CITY POLICE DEPARTMENT

TRAINING ACADEMY. UPON GRADUATION I WAS ASSIGNED TO PATROL IN THE 10TH PRECINCT AND LATER TO THE 90TH PRECINCT, WHERE I WORKED AS A K-9 HANDLER. AFTER FIVE YEARS OF PRECINCT PATROL AND OVER 100 ARRESTS, I APPLIED AND WAS ACCEPTED TO THE NEW YORK CITY POLICE DEPARTMENT HARBOR UNIT.

I HAD BEEN TOLD BY OTHER POLICE OFFICERS THAT BEING ACCEPTED INTO THIS "ELITE" UNIT WOULD BE VERY DIFFICULT TO ACHIEVE. ALMOST IMPOSSIBLE. AND IT WAS. IT WAS DIFFICULT BECAUSE IT WAY VERY POLITICAL. IT WAS MORE A QUESTION OF WHO YOU KNEW AND NOT WHAT YOU KNEW. THE SELECTION PROCESS FOR ENTERING THE HARBOR UNIT HAS HAD, AS I HAVE POINTED OUT IN MY COMPLAINT, A DRAMATIC EFFECT ON MINORITIES. FOR EXAMPLE, MINORITIES IN THE HARBOR UNIT ARE POORLY REPRESENTED. THERE ARE NO LATINO SUPERVISORS, ASIAN SUPERVISORS, BLACK SUPERVISORS, OR FEMALE SUPERVISORS IN THE HARBOR UNIT AND ONLY THE BARE MINIMUM OF MINORITY POLICE OFFICERS, AS REQUIRED BY LAW.

JOINING THE HARBOR UNIT WAS THE TURNING POINT OF MY CAREER. A TURN FOR THE WORST. UP UNTIL THEN, MY REPUTATION AS A POLICE OFFICER WAS COMMENDABLE. SADLY, I AM HERE TODAY TO TELL YOU PUBLICLY THAT: FIRST, DISCRIMINATION IS ALIVE AND WELL AMONG POLICE OFFICERS; SECOND, FILING A COMPLAINT WITH NYPD OEEO WAS A BIGGER MISTAKE THAN JOINING THIS "ELITE" UNIT OF DISCRIMINATION;

THIRD; THE NYPD OEEO IS, IN MY OPINION, INEPT.

THE COMPLAINT THAT I FILED WITH NYPD OEEO REGARDING THE HARBOR UNIT WAS NOT RESOLVED. IN FACT, I DROPPED THE COMPLAINT BECAUSE I LOST CONFIDENCE IN THEIR ABILITY TO ADDRESS THE ISSUES. I CAME TO THE REALIZATION THAT THIS OFFICE WAS MORE IN THE BUSINESS OF FULFILLING A LEGAL REQUIREMENT THAN HELPING YOU.

MY REPORTING DISCRIMINATION TO THE NYPD OEEO WORKED AGAINST ME; BECAUSE FOR THE FIRST TIME IN MY CAREER AS A POLICE OFFICER I RECEIVED A POOR EVALUATION WHILE IN THE HARBOR UNIT. THIS WAS MY CONSOLATION PRIZE FOR FILING A COMPLAINT WITH THE NYPD OEEO. ALL I DESIRED WAS TO BECOME A "PILOT OF A POLICE LAUNCH," LIKE EVERYONE ELSE ASPIRES TO BE IN THE HARBOR UNIT.

THE POOR EVALUATION WAS WRITTEN AS A RESULT OF MY HAVING FILED A COMPLAINT. I SAY THIS WITH CONVICTION BECAUSE THERE WAS PRIOR KNOWLEDGE OF MY INTENT TO FILE A COMPLAINT WITH THE NYPD OEEO. THIS IS RETALIATION. THIS DEED VIOLATED MY CIVIL RIGHTS UNDER SECTION 704(A) OF THE CIVIL RIGHTS ACT OF 1964. ONCE AGAIN, THE NYPD OEEO WAS NOTIFIED AND DID NOTHING TO ADDRESS THIS "ACT OF RETALIATION." ALTHOUGH, I WAS TOLD BY THEM THAT IT WOULD BE INVESTIGATED SEPARATE AND APART FROM MY ORIGINAL COMPLAINT.

I WOULD LIKE TO READ FROM MY ORIGINAL COMPLAINT TO CLARIFY MY IMPETUS FOR FILING WITH OEEO. (PAUSE TO READ PORTION OF ORIGINAL COMPLAINT)

I HAVE SUBMITTED A REQUEST FOR A TRANSFER OUT OF THE HARBOR UNIT. I DESIRE TO MOVE ON BEFORE I BECOME A VICTIM OF A "WITCH HUNT." HOW DOES THIS HAPPEN? WHEN DO SUPERVISORS IN THE POLICE DEPARTMENT ENGAGE IN THIS CONDUCT? SIMPLE, WHEN YOU DO NOT FALL INTO LINE WITH THEIR MENTALITY OF, "I AM A SUPERVISOR AND SO THEREFORE I AM," THEY PUNISH YOU ADMINISTRATIVELY.

I DO NOT, AT THIS TIME, RECOMMEND THAT MINORITY POLICE OFFICERS FILE A COMPLAINT WITH THE NYPD OEEO UNTIL COMMISSIONER BRATTON HAS HAD AN OPPORTUNITY TO EVALUATE THAT OFFICE, RECOMMEND CHANGE AND MAKE IT MORE RESPONSIVE TO ITS STATED PURPOSE. CONVERSELY, IF ANY MINORITY POLICE OFFICER DESIRES AN ASSIGNMENT WITH AN "ELITE" UNIT BEWARE THE PITFALLS. TO THEM YOU MAY STILL ONLY REPRESENT A QUOTA. IN SPITE OF THIS, YOU SHOULD ACHIEVE WHAT YOU DESIRE BECAUSE EDUCATION IS A KEY TO OPPORTUNITY. IT IS NOT THE ANSWER TO THE QUESTION OF EMPLOYMENT DISCRIMINATION, BUT IT IS A FORMIDABLE ALLY.

THIS EPISODE, LADIES AND GENTLEMEN, IS ONLY THE BEGINNING OF MY JOURNEY INTO THE ABYSS. I AM CONCERNED BECAUSE I HAVE NINE AND HALF YEARS TO SERVE AS A NEW YORK CITY POLICE OFFICER AND I WANT TO CONTRIBUTE IN A POSITIVE WAY. SO, I STAND HERE BEFORE YOU TODAY TO ASK FOR YOUR HELP IN RESOLVING MY SEEMINGLY DIFFICULT SITUATION. WHY, BECAUSE I WILL NOT TOLERATE DISCRIMINATION IN ANY FORM AGAINST ANYONE. I AM A NEW YORK CITY POLICE OFFICER. THANK YOU.

CITY OF NEW YORK
POLICE DEPARTMENT

Date: December 8, 1993

To: Deputy Commissioner, Office of Equal Employment Opportunity

From: Police Officer Osvaldo A. Rodriguez
New York City Police Department

Subject: Complaint of Employment Discrimination

I, Police Officer Osvaldo Rodriguez, shield 22155, tax registry 882839, assigned to the New York City Police Department Harbor Unit, (hereinafter referred to as "Harbor Unit") desire to exercise my right to file a complaint of **employment discrimination** in accordance with Patrol Guide procedure 120-12.

This complaint is based upon the overt actions, and deliberate actions that have been preferred against me and that have prevented my progress in terms of opportunities, assignments, seniority, and qualifications.

Harbor Unit

The Harbor Unit has only recently begun an **"Affirmative Action"** program designed to admit minorities. The Harbor Unit has been an exclusive entity, allowing only select ethnic groups to enter. Prior to **"Affirmative Action"**, assignment to the Harbor Unit had more to do with nepotism, favoritism and political association. The Harbor Unit has been slow to reverse this inclination and to change with the times. As with any change there is resistance. The resistance is on the part of the administration and police officers, alike.

Complaint

I have been permanently assigned to the Harbor Unit since April 2, 1990. What I have encountered since then has implications of a continuance towards preventing minorities from realizing their potential. This condition has not been explained, or resolved. As a result, **assignments** have been unfair, preferential and have interfered with my seniority, advancement and qualifications in favor of other police officers that are assigned to the Harbor Unit.

My desire has been to be a **Pilot of a Police Launch**. On July 2, 1993, I obtained a United States Coast Guard License as a Master - Inland of vessels up to 100 gross tons; Mate - Near Coastal of vessels up to 100 gross tons. To achieve this objective I purchased a $600.00 home-study course offered by Houston Marine and spent approximately $180.00 in applications fees to fulfill the Coast Guard licensing requirements. In addition, I spent six months of studious work preparing for the exam on my own time. Furthermore, I attended a one week course offered by the Harbor Unit reviewing for this exam.

Implications

My **seniority** has been placed in jeopardy. There are some police officers assigned to the Harbor Unit with less seniority, less time in the Harbor Unit, and no United States Coast Guard license who have been designated as Pilots.

To illustrate this, I invite your attention to the following tables:

Members of the Service Assigned to
The City of New York
Police Department Harbor Unit

(on the same date as the undersigned)

Pilots of Police Launches 30′ or 52′ Boats	Number of Pilots Holding USCG License
8	1

Members of the Service Assigned to
The City of New York
Police Department Harbor Unit

(assigned to Harbor after the undersigned)

Pilots of Police Launches 30′ or 52′ Boats	Number of Pilots Holding USCG License
4	none

In the past four years that I have spent in Harbor, I know of at least 8 police officers assigned to the Harbor Unit (on the same date as the undersigned), become Pilots. Of the twelve there are

4 who entered the Harbor Unit after the undersigned. To date, of the group of police officers who entered the Harbor Unit (on the same date as the undersigned), only one (1) other police officer has earned the United States Coast Guard license. Of the group who entered into the Harbor unit after the undersigned none have earned the license.

Conclusion

Although, a United States Coast Guard license is not a requirement of the Harbor Unit it is looked upon very favorably by the Commanding Officer, the Police Department and the United States Coast Guard. The license distinguishes a police officer from all the others. For a member of the Harbor Unit it represents a dedication to the Police Department's ideals regarding higher education. To possess this license demonstrates that an individual is prepared to assume additional responsibilities.

On the subject of **opportunity**, I have not heard any reasonable explanation for my delay in becoming a "Pilot of a Police Launch", and so I continue to wait. I believe four years is excessive, unreasonable and requires an explanation. To date no adverse comments about any deficiencies as to my work habits, seamanship, pilotage abilities, knowledge of the post, attitude, or punctuality have been made to me by anyone. Therefore, I have no choice but to conclude that there is more to my situation than meets the eye. I refer this complaint to the Office of Equal Employment Opportunity for a resolution that is equitable and, hopefully will change the outlook for future minority groups who desire to join the Harbor Unit.

Accomplishments

April 2, 1990 - Permanently assigned to the Harbor Unit (see attached copy of memorandum).

November 16, 1990 - Obtained PADI Open Water Diver certification (Student #9012504059).

July 2, 1993 - Earned the United States Coast Guard License (serial # 725243) as a Master - Inland of Vessels up to 100 gross tons and; Mate - Near Coastal of Vessels up to 100 gross tons.

Military

June 1972 - Present (reserve) Completed 20 years of military service in the United States Naval Reserve. Presently assigned to the Mine Inshore Undersea Warfare Unit 203, Floyd Bennett Field, Brooklyn, New York. I currently hold the rank of Radioman First Class (E-6) and have been recommended for the rank of Chief Petty Officer. My responsibilities include: <u>Watch Supervisor</u> of TQS-108 van, (a mobile radar, sonar, and communications equipped platform, capable of surface and sub-surface surveillance). During my active duty time (June 1972 - June 1975), I was assigned as a <u>Boatswain Mate</u> on-board the Aircraft Carrier, USS Forrestal, CVA-59. Qualified as <u>Helmsman</u> - Underway/Flight Operations. Promoted to Radioman 3rd Class in 1973.

Currently hold a TOP-SECRET CLEARANCE with the United States Navy.

Status

Married, two children

Chairman OWENS. Thank you.

You are a New York City police officer. You are an American citizen. You should not have to scale back your ambitions and your desire to serve in an elite unit because you are a minority, but that is the case. Your testimony shows a great deal of personal pain. We hope to help end that kind of pattern.

The fact that is you are involved in agencies which are vital, that hold critical positions in our society, and we should be able to look to the law enforcement agencies to at least keep up with the rest of society. From the testimony that we have heard, it appears that our law enforcement agencies are behind and as slow as things are moving with regard to affirmative action and equal opportunity elsewhere, it seems that law enforcement agencies are behind everybody else.

With the old-boy networks and the paramilitary structures, they are able to pretty much preserve what existed 20 years ago. As two people testified this morning, this is not very different from what it was 20 years ago.

After all the lawsuits, consent decrees and all the action that has been taken, it appears that things have stayed as they were. However, if there hadn't been some activity, things would have gotten much worse.

It is a very serious business. Most of you are old enough to remember the Connor Report that investigated the riots that took place in the 1960s and came to the conclusion that it is always action by the police which sparks the explosive violent activity.

People have numerous grievances, and those grievances pile up, but they are not the only reasons why you had the riots and the rebellions. Actions by the police always triggered it because police are symbols of authority, symbols of establishment. They always triggered the explosion.

So if the police cannot be reformed from within, if they are not reflective of the pursuit of justice that society as a whole wants to undertake, then we are in a hopeless situation.

I think that there are several approaches that can be taken in addition to pushing the EEOC and the Justice Department at the Federal level to pursue law enforcement agencies as a priority class action case. I serve on the Education and Labor Committee, and there is a question of the PBA's in situations where PBA's are closed shops by law. You must pay your dues to the PBA.

I am not certain that they are regulated by the National Labor Relations Board in the way other unions are regulated.

I am not certain if they are required to follow the same kinds of practices. There is room for investigation there. If you can't get decent attorneys in your own internal procedure—the kind of service that you pay for with your dues—then you are at a great disadvantage in terms of using the due process procedures that are set up, as inadequate as those procedures may be.

I want to thank you again for all the support that you have given by appearing here to testify today. I would like to ask a few questions.

Has there ever been any legal challenge of the Patrolmen's Benevolent Association in their representation practices and their failure to represent minorities?

Mr. RODRIGUEZ. Not to my knowledge.

Ms. WHITE-RUIZ. According to PBA, they are there. They claim they are there to represent you and to advise you. What they do advise you to do is to take whatever punishment they are willing to give you as long as you keep your job.

What they don't tell you is that if you get 30 days' suspension in a year or probation, anything that you do will result in your dismissal. They are present in body, not in spirit. They are advising you but they are not advising you correctly as far as I am concerned.

If you have something to stand up for and the PBA attorney is telling you to shut your mouth and take what they give you, that is not advice. That is a pattern.

In some cases where you have a witness, they will refuse to allow them to take the witness stand. In the kangaroo courts, it doesn't matter; your witness is not recognized. In some cases, some of your evidence disappears.

As far as getting a PBA minority, I have 209 officers in the 90th Precinct; 54 are minorities. You cannot win a vote on that.

Chairman OWENS. Have you pursued through your Guardians Association——

Ms. WHITE-RUIZ. Based on the practices of the New York City Police Department, because there are not that many minorities hired, when a class graduates, you will get four in one precinct, one in another, and three over here. They will never add up to an equal amount of minorities versus whites.

Chairman OWENS. I understand that. I want to pursue another point in terms of the Guardians themselves taking certain kinds of action, with your limited resources.

Mr. SANDERS. When Grace and I took office, we were aware that Philadelphia sued their PBA or their union under the Fair Duty Misrepresentation Act, which is a Federal law. We studied the feasibility of doing that also.

Chairman OWENS. Has anybody ever pointed out this disparity in punishment situation and proposed some kind of system which would correct it? In the age of computers, we ought to be able to find out all the punishments that have been meted out and enter them in terms of race, sex, et cetera, and be able to find out what the pattern is.

Is there disparity in punishment so that a black police officer gets 15 days for something that a white police officer gets five days for? We ought to be able to statistically evaluate that if they keep records.

Ms. WHITE-RUIZ. That is pointed out, but nobody outside has a say-so as far as how the kangaroo court is run.

Mr. SANDERS. What we asked for—Grace and I asked for that information. We tried to use a track of three years, from 1990 to 1993, requesting all this information about OEO complaints. I asked for specifically for a breakdown by race, by educational background, et cetera. They were supposed to respond back to us by May 26. It is now June 13 and they haven't responded.

84-118 - 94 - 4

So I have to go back on my computer and write another nice letter to them telling them we are going to sue to get the information because they should have released it to us. We are trying to do it back three years. We should do it back 20 years, but we have limited resources. It would just be too much paperwork.

It is very easy—when you look at those personnel orders and you see the names and you know the police officers and you see police officer lost his gun, dismissed. Another police officer lost his gun, another five days. Another police officer lost his gun; 15 days.

Police Officer Sanders, perjury; 20 days, a year's suspension. Police officer so-and-so, another command, I know another police officer that they accused of this, who has Mafia ties.

Ms. LILLY-ELMORE. We have done the same thing in the Department of Correction, to no avail.

Chairman OWENS. We should bring the impact of government agencies into doing this in a more thorough way to at least get the facts on the table and make the comparative analysis.

We have run out of time. I would like to give each of you an opportunity to make one last comment.

Ms. WHITE-RUIZ. I would like to make one proposal.

There have been numerous lawsuits filed against the New York City Police Department and particular people in question. I would like to propose that instead of the New York City Police Department covering for these people, let them be responsible for the monetary value they are being sued for.

If they find out that they are responsible for paying up to $500,000 to an individual for crimes committed against them, they will no longer commit these crimes.

Once they are being sued and individuals that are being sued, the Police Department will pay for them, so this enables them to continue what they have done because they have to pay nothing out of their pocket. They are not hurt in any way.

Mr. SANDERS. Maybe you need to revise the general Municipal Law 50(k) which covers civil liability for police officers, because that's another way to get a police officer out of trouble. They know they have committed a wrongdoing so they don't give them charges and specifications or any kind of CD; that way, they can cover them.

Someone on a higher level should look at different cases and look at how to use Municipal Law 50(k) because it costs the State of New York millions of dollars every year to settle lawsuits with the New York City Police Department because of abuse of authority, racism, sexism, harassment and maybe assaults against citizens.

Chairman OWENS. Will you explain what a CD is?

Mr. SANDERS. Command discipline.

Ms. RIDLEY. I would like to propose that we look into the Department of Personnel, their hiring practices, how they hire, how they make recommendations on promotions, their criteria. I think that what needs to happen is that the way the promotions come about, the way that hiring comes about, should be taken from the Department of Personnel.

Somebody should be an overseer of the Department of Personnel because African-Americans and minorities are not getting a fair shake in that sense.

Chairman OWENS. Thank you very much.

If you have any further comments, please submit them to the subcommittee within the next 10 days.

The hearing is now adjourned.

[Whereupon, at 1:40 p.m., the subcommittee was adjourned.]

[Additional material submitted for the record follows:]

Statement of Russell Smith, New York City Police Department, Flushing, New York

Subcommittee on Select Education and Civil Rights:

As a Guardian member of the City of New York Police Department, I would like to share some of my experiences as a black police officer. I was appointed on July 16, 1984 to the New York City Police Department [NYCPD]. On January 11, 1986, I became the first black helicopter pilot in NYCPD history with the assistance of: the former Police Commissioner Benjamin Ward, Chief of Department Robert J. Johnson Jr., and the Guardian Association for Black Police Officers.

Historically, the Aviation unit was as elite white unit of Pilots and Mechanics from October 21, 1929 until my arrival on January 11, 1986. Prior to entering the unit, efforts were made to prevent any black pilots from entering this elite unit. In the past, there were qualified blacks with military pilot experience who were turned down due to the color of their skin.

I was qualified to enter the unit with my pilot license and experience. While serving in this unit I experienced situations where certain officers stayed away from me and at times has a hard time keeping their bias opinions to themselves. Prior to reporting to the unit a supervisor had to sit down with the officers to inform them that they had to welcome their first black pilot and to keep their racial and bias opinions and remarks to themselves. I was assigned to a young white officer who was my flight instructor fortunately, he was the only pilot willing [at that time] to teach me the helicopter flight operations. After obtaining my additional helicopter pilot ratings I advanced through the system with hard work and commitment.

There were times when I was passed over for additional NYCPD flight operations training and rating opportunities in which I was passed over by white officers with less training and time in the Aviation Unit. In the past I had filed an EEO complaint against a supervisor who discriminated against me. Throughout my seven years in this unit racism, harassment, and retaliation is the norm for this unit. I am an outspoken person who stood up to racism and had paid a price for it. It is a constant challenge to fight the racism, harassment, and retaliation in the NYCPD.

On many occasions I have observed other incidents of racism, harassment and retaliation in other specialized units within the NYCPD system. There is no question in my mind that the NYCPD infrastructure do not support blacks. I know a black female who has a pilot license and excellent credentials who was not permitted to enter the elite Aviation Unit. This applicant's first interview, [which I had first-hand knowledge of] was successful; however, a new administration came in and requested a second interview and made her feel unworthy.

At this time, I have a Federal lawsuit against the New York City Police Department in the U.S. District Court—Eastern Division index #CV940271 assigned to Judge Reena Raggi for discrimination, harassment, and retaliation.

Statement of Lanny E. Walter, Attorney, for David Jemmott, Jr., New York Department of Correctional Services, New York

I write on behalf of David Jemmott, Jr., and African-American correction officer for 14 years, employed by the New York State Department of Correctional Services at Mt. McGregor Correctional Facility in Saratoga County, NY.

Mr. Jemmott emeplifies the professional within the criminal justice system who is the victim of racism. Out of a security staff of a few hundred, there are two African-Americans permanently assigned to Mt. McGregor, a medium/minimum prison. Most African-Americans temporarily assigned to that prison quickly transfer out to a less hostile environment.

Only Mr. Jemmott and one other officer with family roots in that part of the State have persevered despite the atmosphere of racial bias.

Mr. Jemmott has had to endure the "nigger" taunts directed both at himself and at prisoners by white officers who have never learned to treat all persons as equals.

David Jemmott has refused to accept the racism. When a Jesse Jackson campaign poster is defaced to convey a racial insult, he reports it to the warden. When the union office in the prison displays a cartoon of an electric chair over which was written "Nigger Sparker," he demands that it be removed. The "good ole boys," known at Mt. McGregor as the "palsies," resent Mr. Jemmott's insistence that they curb their racist attitudes.

As a result, he has incurred the hostility of the palsies and they play their stupid games against him. They file false disciplinary charges; they tell him in front of a group of African-American prisoners that he should remember his place in this white institution; they make threatening telephone calls to his home reminding him,

"Tar baby, don't forget Donna Payant" [a female correction officer who was killed at Green Haven Correctional Facility]; they permit him to take a day off and then accuse him of being AWOL; they give him assignments that do not reflect his seniority and fail to give him the same assistance on that job as is given to other C.O.s, placing his life in jeopardy; and they even search his person in front of prisoners.

David Jemmott is living a racial nightmare at Mt. McGregor. He does not want to quit. A C.O. receives good pay and benefits. He does not want to transfer to another prison. Mt. McGregor is the most convenient prison to where he resides. Why should he have to move? Why should he give in to their racist behavior?

Mr. Jemmott has brought his difficulties at Mt. McGregor to the attention of senior officials at the Department of Correctional Services. They are unwilling to root out the problem. The racist environment can only change by a full scale commitment to integrate the work forces at all NYS prisons. The prisons near NYC have large numbers of African-American and Hispanic employees. The prisons in the north country are almost exclusively white.

New York State runs a segregated penal system. David Jemmott urges the Federal Government to undertake a desegregation effort. The demeaning treatmemt to which he is subjected would not continue in a work force including substantial numbers of minorities who would not tolerate such bigotry.

CITY OF NEW YORK
POLICE DEPARTMENT
DEPUTY COMMISSIONER, LEGAL MATTERS
ONE POLICE PLAZA
NEW YORK, N.Y. 10038

JUL 19 1994

June 30, 1994

Representative Major R. Owens
Chairperson, House Subcommittee on
Select Education and Civil Rights
U.S. House of Representatives
518 House Annex I
Washington, D.C. 20515-6107

Dear Representative Owens:

I am writing to you on behalf of New York City Police Commissioner William J. Bratton, who was unable to attend your recent Subcommittee hearing at New York City Technical College. I am pleased to forward to you personnel data for the New York City Police Department as of May 31, 1994, categorized by gender, race, and ethnicity. We have also prepared tables comparing the data to corresponding staffing levels of January, 1990.

I trust that this information will prove useful. Please do not hesitate to contact me with any questions which you may have regarding the data.

Very truly yours,

JEREMY TRAVIS
Deputy Commissioner
Legal Matters

att.
cc: Director, New York City
Washington, D.C. Office

STATISTICS FOR NEW YORK CITY POLICE DEPARTMENT BY GENDER, ETHNICITY AND RANK

STATISTICS BY GENDER AND ETHNICITY (TOTAL DEPARTMENT)

TOTAL	MALE	FEMALE
40,805 (100%)	28,648 (70.2%)	12,157 (29.8%)

TOTAL	WHITE	BLACK	HISP	ASIAN	NAT.AM.
40,805 (100%)	25,513 (62.5%)	8,662 (21.2%)	6,042 (14.8%)	532 (1.3%)	56 (.1%)

STATISTICS BY GENDER AND ETHNICITY (UNIFORM)

TOTAL	MALE	FEMALE
30,795 (100%)	26,331 (85.5%)	4,464 (14.5%)

TOTAL	WHITE	BLACK	HISP	ASIAN	NAT.AM.
30,795 (100%)	22,260 (72.3%)	3,560 (11.6%)	4,623 (15.0%)	313 (1.0%)	39 (.1%)

STATISTICS BY GENDER AND ETHNICITY (CIVILIAN)

TOTAL	MALE	FEMALE
10,010 (100%)	2,317 (23.1%)	7,693 (76.9%)

TOTAL	WHITE	BLACK	HISP	ASIAN	NAT.AM.
10,010 (100%)	3,253 (32.5%)	5,102 (51.0%)	1,419 (14.3%)	219 (2.2%)	17 (.2%)

CONTINUED - NYPD STATISTICS BY GENDER, ETHNICITY AND RANK

STATISTICS FOR GENDER AND ETHNICITY BY RANK (UNIFORM)

	TOTAL	MALE	FEMALE
PO'S & DETS.	25,842 (100%)	21,724 (84.1%)	4,118 (15.9%)

TOTAL	WHITE	BLACK	HISP	ASIAN	NAT.AM.
25,842 (100%)	17,975 (69.6%)	3,246 (12.6%)	4,305 (16.7%)	279 (1.1%)	37 (.1%)

	TOTAL	MALE	FEMALE
SGTS.	3,331 (100%)	3,058 (91.8%)	273 (8.2%)

TOTAL	WHITE	BLACK	HISP	ASIAN	NAT.AM.
3,331 (100%)	2,815 (84.5%)	240 (7.2%)	247 (7.4%)	27 (.8%)	2 (.1%)

	TOTAL	MALE	FEMALE
LTS.	1,130 (100%)	1,072 (94.9%)	58 (5.1%)

TOTAL	WHITE	BLACK	HISP	ASIAN	NAT.AM.
1,130 (100%)	995 (88.1%)	66 (5.8%)	63 (5.6%)	6 (.5%)	0 (0%)

CONTINUED - NYPD STATISTICS BY GENDER, ETHNICITY AND RANK

	TOTAL	MALE	FEMALE			
CAPTS.	312 (100%)	301 (96.5%)	11 (3.5%)			
	TOTAL	**WHITE**	**BLACK**	**HISP**	**ASIAN**	**NAT.AM.**
	312 (100%)	307 (98.4%)	1 (.3%)	3 (1.0%)	1 (.3%)	0 (0%)

	TOTAL	MALE	FEMALE			
ABOVE CAPT.	180 (100%)	176 (97.8%)	4 (2.2%)			
	TOTAL	**WHITE**	**BLACK**	**HISP**	**ASIAN**	**NAT.AM.**
	180 (100%)	168 (93.3%)	7 (3.9%)	5 (2.8%)	0 (0%)	0 (0%)

NYPD TOTAL
UNIFORMED PERSONNEL (ALL RANKS)
BY SEX & ETHNICITY

	May 1994	January 1990	Difference #	+/- %	May 94 Proportions	Jan. 90 Proportions
White	22,260	19,559	+2,701	+13.8%	72.3%	76.6%
Black	3,560	2,833	+727	+25.7%	11.6%	11.1%
Hispanic	4,623	2,955	+1,668	+56.4%	15.0%	11.6%
Other	352	196	+156	+79.6%	1.1%	0.8%
Male	26,331	22,318	+4,013	+18.0%	85.5%	87.4%
Female	4,464	3,225	+1,239	+38.4%	14.5%	12.6%
M/White	20,064	17,774	+2,290	+12.9%	65.2%	69.6%
M/Black	2,310	1,958	+352	+18.0%	7.5%	7.7%
M/Hispanic	3,644	2,415	+1,229	+50.9%	11.8%	9.5%
M/Other	313	171	+142	+83.0%	1.0%	0.7%
F/White	2,196	1,785	+411	+23.0%	7.1%	7.0%
F/Black	1,250	875	+375	+42.9%	4.1%	3.4%
F/Hispanic	979	540	+439	+81.3%	3.2%	2.1%
F/Other	39	25	+14	+56.0%	0.1%	0.1%
TOTAL UNIFORMED	30,795	25,543	+5,252	+20.6%	100.0%	100.0%

- Blacks increased +25.7%, now account for 11.6% of all Uniformed Personnel

- Hispanics increased +56.4%, now account for 15.0% of all Uniformed Personnel

- Females increased +38.4%, now account for 14.5% of all Uniformed Personnel

NYPD
POLICE OFFICERS
BY SEX & ETHNICITY

	May 1994	January 1990	Difference #	+/- %	May 94 Proportions	Jan. 90 Proportions
White	15,616	13,256	+2,360	+17.8%	70.3%	75.0%
Black	2,641	2,006	+635	+31.7%	11.9%	11.3%
Hispanic	3,703	2,275	+1,428	+62.8%	16.7%	12.9%
Other	260	143	+117	+81.8%	1.2%	0.8%
Male	18,641	15,071	+3,570	+23.7%	83.9%	85.2%
Female	3,579	2,609	+970	+37.2%	16.1%	14.8%
M/White	13,938	11,835	+2,103	+17.8%	62.7%	66.9%
M/Black	1,597	1,296	+301	+23.2%	7.2%	7.3%
M/Hispanic	2,880	1,819	+1,061	+58.3%	13.0%	10.3%
M/Other	226	121	+105	+86.8%	1.0%	0.7%
F/White	1,678	1,421	+257	+18.1%	7.6%	8.0%
F/Black	1,044	710	+334	+47.0%	4.7%	4.0%
F/Hispanic	823	456	+367	+80.5%	3.7%	2.6%
F/Other	34	22	+12	+54.5%	0.2%	0.1%
TOTAL UNIFORMED	22,220	17,680	+4,540	+25.7%	100.0%	100.0%

- Blacks increased +31.7%, now account for 11.9% of all Police Officers
- Hispanics increased +62.8%, now account for 16.7% of all Police Officers
- Females increased +37.2%, now account for 16.1% of all Police Officers

NYPD
DETECTIVES (ALL GRADES)
BY SEX & ETHNICITY

	May 1994	January 1990	Difference #	+/- %	May 94 Proportions	Jan. 90 Proportions
White	2,359	2,324	+35	+1.5%	65.1%	70.9%
Black	605	494	+111	+22.5%	16.7%	15.1%
Hispanic	602	423	+179	+42.3%	16.6%	12.9%
Other	58	38	+20	+52.6%	1.6%	1.2%
Male	3,083	2,893	+190	+6.6%	85.1%	88.3%
Female	539	385	+154	+40.0%	14.9%	11.7%
M/White	2,104	2,135	-31	-1.5%	58.1%	65.1%
M/Black	450	372	+78	+21.0%	12.4%	11.3%
M/Hispanic	477	352	+125	+35.5%	13.2%	10.7%
M/Other	52	34	+18	+52.9%	1.4%	1.0%
F/White	255	189	+66	+34.9%	7.0%	5.8%
F/Black	155	122	+33	+27.0%	4.3%	3.7%
F/Hispanic	125	71	+54	+76.1%	3.5%	2.2%
F/Other	4	3	+1	+33.3%	0.1%	0.1%
TOTAL UNIFORMED	3,622	3,278	+344	+10.5%	100.1%	100.0%

o Blacks increased +22.5%, now account for 16.7% of all Detectives

o Hispanics increased +42.3%, now account for 16.6% of all Detectives

o Females increased +40.0%, now account for 14.9% of all Detectives

NYPD
ALL SERGEANTS
BY SEX & ETHNICITY

	May 1994	January 1990	Difference #	+/- %	May 94 Proportions	Jan. 90 Proportions
White	2,815	2,443	+372	+15.2%	84.5%	82.4%
Black	240	286	-46	-16.1%	7.2%	9.6%
Hispanic	247	222	+25	+11.3%	7.4%	7.5%
Other	29	14	+15	+107.1%	0.9%	0.5%
Male	3,058	2,778	+280	+10.1%	91.8%	93.7%
Female	273	187	+86	+46.0%	8.2%	6.3%
M/White	2,614	2,308	+306	+13.3%	78.5%	77.8%
M/Black	198	246	-48	-19.5%	5.9%	8.3%
M/Hispanic	218	210	+8	+3.8%	6.5%	7.1%
M/Other	28	14	+14	+100.0%	0.8%	0.5%
F/White	201	135	+66	+48.9%	6.0%	4.6%
F/Black	42	40	+2	+5.0%	1.3%	1.3%
F/Hispanic	29	12	+17	+141.7%	0.9%	0.4%
F/Other	1	0	+1	N/A	0.0%	0.0%
TOTAL UNIFORMED	3,331	2,965	+366	+12.3%	100.0%	100.0%

o Blacks decreased -16.1%, now account for 7.2% of all Sergeants

o Hispanics increased +11.3%, now account for 7.4% of all Sergeants

o Females increased +46.0%, now account for 8.2% of all Sergeants

NYPD
ALL LIEUTENANTS
BY SEX & ETHNICITY

	May 1994	January 1990	Difference #	+/- %	May 94 Proportions	Jan. 90 Proportions
White	995	1,038	-43	-4.1%	88.1%	93.8%
Black	66	39	+27	+69.2%	5.8%	3.5%
Hispanic	63	28	+35	+125.0%	5.6%	2.5%
Other	6	2	+4	+200.0%	0.5%	0.2%
Male	1,072	1,066	+6	+0.6%	94.9%	96.3%
Female	58	41	+17	+41.5%	5.1%	3.7%
M/White	947	1,001	-54	-5.4%	83.8%	90.4%
M/Black	58	36	+22	+61.1%	5.1%	3.3%
M/Hispanic	61	27	+34	+125.9%	5.4%	2.4%
M/Other	6	2	+4	+200.0%	0.5%	0.2%
F/White	48	37	+11	+29.7%	4.2%	3.3%
F/Black	8	3	+5	+166.7%	0.7%	0.3%
F/Hispanic	2	1	+1	+100.0%	0.2%	0.1%
F/Other	0	0	0	N/A	0.0%	0.0%
TOTAL UNIFORMED	1,130	1,107	+23	+2.1%	100.0%	100.0%

o Blacks increased +69.2%, now account for 5.8% of all Lieutenants

o Hispanics increased +125.0%, now account for 5.6% of all Lieutenants

o Females increased +41.5%, now account for 5.1% of all Lieutenants

NYPD
ALL CAPTAINS AND ABOVE
BY SEX & ETHNICITY

	May 1994	January 1990	Difference #	+/- %	May 94 Proportions	Jan. 90 Proportions
White	475	498	-23	-4.6%	96.5%	97.1%
Black	8	8	0	0.0%	1.6%	1.6%
Hispanic	8	7	+1	+14.3%	1.6%	1.4%
Other	1	0	+1	N/A	0.2%	0.0%
Male	477	510	-33	-6.5%	97.0%	99.4%
Female	15	3	+12	+400.0%	3.0%	0.6%
M/White	461	495	-34	-6.9%	93.7%	96.5%
M/Black	7	8	-1	-12.5%	1.4%	1.6%
M/Hispanic	8	7	+1	+14.3%	1.6%	1.4%
M/Other	1	0	+1	N/A	0.2%	0.0%
F/White	14	3	+11	+366.7%	2.8%	0.6%
F/Black	1	0	+1	N/A	0.2%	0.0%
F/Hispanic	0	0	0	N/A	0.0%	0.0%
F/Other	0	0	0	N/A	0.0%	0.0%
TOTAL UNIFORMED	492	513	-21	-4.1%	100.0%	100.0%

o Blacks did not change, now account for 1.6% of all Captains and higher ranks

o Hispanics increased +14.3%, now account for 1.6% of all Captains and higher ranks

o Females increased +400.0%, now account for 3.0% of all Captains and higher ranks

EGIDIO SEMENTILLE
2041 Colonial Avenue
Bronx, NY 10461
212-364-6486
212-733-5694 FAX

TO: Hon. Congressman Major Owens
Sub-Committee investigating minority discrimination in law enforcement agencies
718-735-7143

RE: Pending Article 78 Petition attached hereto requires further investigation
your Sub-Committee. I can furnish many witnesses to institutionalized applied discrimination based upon entrenched academic fraud honed to support minority enslavement and discrimination.

If I can be of further assistance, please contact me.

Sincerely yours,

EGIDIO SEMENTILLE

SUPREME COURT OF THE STATE OF NEW YORK
COUNTY OF NEW YORK

- - - - - - - - - - - - - - - - - - - -x

IN THE MATTER OF
THE APPLICATION OF

EGIDIO SEMENTILLI,

Petitioner,

FOR A JUDGMENT UNDER ARTICLE 78 OF
THE CIVIL PRACTICE LAW AND RULES
IN THE NATURE OF MANDAMUS

-against-

RUDOLPH GIULIANI, MAYOR OF NEW YORK,
WILLIAM BRATTON, NEW YORK CITY POLICE COMMISSIONER
BERNARD H. JACKSON, CHAIRMAN CIVIL SERVICE COMMISSION
LILIAM BARRIOS-PAOLI, DIRECTOR DEPARTMENT PERSONNELL
RAYMOND D. FOWLER, PRESIDENT AMERICAN PSYCHOLOGICAL ASSOCIATION
JEERY WIENER, PRESIDENT AMERICAN PSYCHIATRIC ASSOCIATION

Respondents.

- - - - - - - - - - - - - - - - - - - -x

PETITION IN SUPPORT OF AN
ARTICLE 78 PETITION; ALTERNATIVE DECLARATORY JUDGMENT RELIEF

INDEX: 94115646

STATE OF NEW YORK)
COUNTY OF NEW YORK) ss:

EGIDIO SEMENTILLI, being duly swrn deposes and says:

1. I am the Petitioner herein and I make this petition to request this Court to Order the respondents William Bratton, Commissioner of the New York City Police Department to hire petitioner and to order the Department of Personnel to cease and desist in the use of so-called psychological and psychiatric "testing" to violate petitioner's civil rights as a substitute for anti-Italian Roman Catholic discrimination based upon institutionalized hatred of said minority, and/or other victimized minorities.

2. Jurisdiction is in this Court is based upon the place of doing business of the respondents in the County of New York directly or through proxies, agents and adherents of the procedures applied in violation petitioner's civil rights and denial of petitioner's right to due process of law. Petitioner is a resident of Bronx County, New York and that the respondents are a body or officer of a body as defined in Article 78 Section 7802. Additionally CPLR 3001 relief by way of additional and/or altemtive relief is sought because respondents have wilfully, maliciously, in bad faith sought to deny petitioner his constitutional rights by usurpation of office for financially lucrative purposes to the damage of petitioner and other similarly situated.

3. Petitioner applied to take the Police Officer placement examination No. 9006 and successfully received notice that he was placed on the eligible list with No. 3793. Thereafter he was required to submit to purported "purported psychological evaluation".

4. The "psychological evaluation" was in fact a religious ritual similar to historical rituals ***of the "devil worship" sect.*** *The ritual was conducted by the application of the "Minnesota Multi-Phasic Personality Inventory", the "Cornell Index" and the "California Psychological In ventory" and the "House Tree Projective Test" written material in addition to a Police Candidate Questionnaire and Biographical Date Sheet,which included a section in which he was asked to describe his most stressful experience.also an oral interview with a "psychologist" rite master. Administrative review was denied on February 2,1994 and this proceeding is commenced within 120 days from said determination.*

5. Petitioner had previously been fully qualified psychologically, physically and character qualification on examination No. 5114. Due to budget cuts petitioner was invited to be sworn into service on two previous occasions. On the first occasion Petitioner received a telephone notice not to appear for oath of employment due to budget cancellation of the planned recruitment effort. Petitioner was sent for a second psychological ritual under examination No.5114 due to a two year lapse and was notified that he was ritually disqualified.

6. Petitioner submitted eleven letters of recommendation and ritually evaluated by Dr. Harvey Schlossberg, PhD. in an administrative review supporting petitioner's psychological qualifications for employment which efforts were rejected by respondents.

7. Petitioner took the instant examination and was ritually disqualified by the metaphor of "devil worship" rites that are a fraudulent academic concoction as herein explained and that all actions by the respondents responsive to petitioner's employment are arbitrary, capricious, unreasonable and in addition are ridiculous by their very nature and supportive of disloyal efforts to make a mockery of public institutions and the duly constituted authority, all of which are illegal and in violation of petitioner's constitutional rights.

8. The above stated "rituals" do not conform to the standards set by the Supreme Court of the ***United States*** *in Doubert v. Merrell Pharmaceitical,* ***Docket No. 92-102 and are inherently*** *fraudulent and illegal religious posture in violation of the* ***First, Fifth, Sixth, Thirteenth and Fourteenth Amendments*** *to the Constitution.*

9. The respondents American Psychiatric Association, by Jerry Wiener, its president is engaged directly and indirectly through proxies, agents and collaborators in and out of the public sector to "conscript" the mind and body as a mask to protect entrenched economic and political interests as a metaphor to implement modalities of involuntary servitude in its deceptive cosmetic efforts manifested by a "bill of attainder" of social stigmatization and condemnation to life long punishment in under paid employment to be applied in a manner to circumvent prohibitions of ethno-religious discrimination inherent in institutionalized anti-Italian Roman Catholicism. Respondent American Psychological Association is similarly active and responsible for the organized racketeering in fraudulent academic and related public and private efforts all in ***violation of 18 USC 1961 et seq. 11 USC 4, 42 USC 1981 to 1985.***

10. The respondent New York City Police Department institutionalized the ritual "testing" procedures so that the Police Department could attempt to "legally" though fraudulently circumvent laws prohibiting enthno-racial discrimination put in place with broad ***civil rights enforcement legislation of the 1960's in state and federal legislation.***

11. The respondent New York City Civil Service Commission is a redundant, fraudulent public relations damage control effort to usurp and conceal entrenched Police Department protected discrimination and inherent Police Department corruption in its media referenced efforts for which judicial notice is demand and required. Remedial policies to increase minority representation are systematically defeated and circumvented by the pseudo-medical religious and religious and ritualistic psychological "test" screening procedures honed to perpetuate entrenched patterns of personnel recruitment.

12.The Department of Personnel, the oversight agency for the New York City Civil Service Commission has illegally, but under color of law, delegated its function to the respondents New York City Civil Service Commission, New York City Police Department in order circumvent laws prohibiting ethno-racial discrimination and as a substitution for the rule of law in a racketeering extraneous to the legislatively delegated authority.

13. The respondents substitution of academic fraud in a pattern of racketeering clearly articulated in the annexed exhibit, being a decision of the respondent New York City Civil Service Commission dismissing petitioner's administrative appeal by relying on its fraudulently conceived and applied allegation of petitioner's failure of "medical documentation" under Rule 60 R. NYC 2-02(g). This decision attempts to legalize the academic fraud and racketeering to support the vested economic and institutional interest in substitution for the constitutional rights of petitioner in violation of law. ***See St Francis College v. AlKhazraji 481 US 604 and Shaare Tefila v. Cobb 481 US 615.***

14 The attempt to equate "psychological" with medical evidence is false, fraudulent and a ridiculous mockery of the rational human capacity. Alleged "Psychological" testing referred to herein is undistinguishable from traditional religion in violation of the stated constitutional provisions. Hence, the illegality of the "religious" test also brings down the illegality of the respondents' alleged reliance on Rule 4.3.3 of the Rules and Regulations of the City Personnel Director. Psychology, psychiatry, and psychoanalysis are inherently anti-semitic and anti-Roman Catholic because they the said ideologies reject the scriptural premises for the Messianic redemption of Jewish existence and deny Roman Catholics the absolution of sin. This is so because the purported "procedures" are efforts to examine petitioner's soul. By definition "psychology" etc are the study or cure of the soul. "Soul" is the abstract essence of the human condition of only metaphysical dimension. Simply stated the soul is beyond objective scientific measurement.

15. The ridiculous nature of the respondents institutionalized totalitarian arbitrary, unreasonable and capricious action here sought to be corrected are made clearer if petitioner sought to submit to traditional confession to a Roman Catholic priest for the benefit of the health of petitioner's soul as his fundamental effort to prove his burden of "psychological" adequacy. Such an effort would be tainted by prohibitions of morality in public employment as a substitute condition for what is called by respondents "psychological" qualification.

16. In addition to the mischievous unreasonableness, etc. cited above vagueness of concept and application thereof are inherent in the purported "standards" compiled not by listening to petitioner's "psyche" but by a committee of known and unknown editors and "test" makers and readers who discredit the "medical" compliance of petitioner as evidenced by petitioner's blood, urine, tissue, skin, mucous, cartilage, bones and vital.

*17. The dehumanizing respondents' malice is proven by the **vagueness.** of its procedures. **Vagueness** is an inhuman demand upon the applicant for employment that makes it impossible for him/her to form an intentional act in response to an external event or circumstance(s) in a responsible manner consistent with the human condition. The lack of clarity makes it impossible to form a mental intent to proceed upon a given course of responsive action.*

*18. **Vagueness** is inherent in the formation of an opinion, in the instant case, that opinion is honed to apply patterns of illegal ethno-racial hatred protocols of discrimination akin to the conditions of inhuman servitude **outlawed by the Thirteenth Amendment.** This servitude inherent in vagueness, opinion and other fraud is dealt with in **US v. Reynolds 98 US 145 which establishes the rule that the "Civil magistrate may not intrude into the field of opinion. This language is taken from the "Virginia Statute of Religious Freedoms" prohibiting government** intrusion where no objective validity can be proven. This describes psychiatry and psychology, but not neurology where a dispute of the existence of a brain tumor may be resolved by an X-Ray picture or microscopic tissue slide.*

*19. Respondents reliance upon DSM 3R (Diagnostic and Statistical Manual, Third Edition Revised) is institutionalized academic fraud couched-self serving fraudulent grant and financial payments efforts for public and private money rather than the validity of the applicant's mental condition for performance of the employment opportunity in view of the applicant. Hence any "statistical" theses as a standard of petitioner's employability must be disregarded as violative of the Sixth Amendment right to confront and examine witnesses in this quasi criminal nature of psychological stigmatization "bill of attainder" punishment as a metaphor of **"Devil worship"** and the application of the cult of **"stigmata diaboli" or devil's marks of medieval origins.***

20. The purported "authority" for respondents hatred protocol is not derived from any "democratic" disposition of the duly constituted authority or its proxies, agents or delegates but by from fraudulently conceived academic cartels operating by usurpation of power, not elected to office in a manner consistent with democratic procedures, by educational, scientific or charitable institutions for self serving purposes in violation and substitution of duly constituted legal institutions and structures.

21. Petitioner is entitled to declaratory judgment relief and enforcement in consequence of the bad faith and wilful discrimination of the petitioner in violation of his constitutional right to equal protection of the law without having to pass a "religious test" for such relief set forth above.

*WHEREFORE, petitioner demands that the respondents cease and desist and be forever enjoined from using and enforcing its purported racketeer, hatred and discriminatory procedures in violation of petitioner's civil and constitutional rights, including the similar rights of others similarly situated and that the New York City Police Department psychological unit, or effort honed to practice ethno racial discriminatory procedure, be forever abolished that the respondents be ordered to employ petitioner with restoration of retroactive salaries, earnings, promotional opportunities applicable to seniority retroactively applied to July 11, 1990, examination No. 5114 list No. 15,714, and further, and alternatively to the application of the said constitutional and civil rights of the petitioner to a declaratory judgement pursuant to CPLR 3001 and 3002 sustaining action notwithstanding inconsistency in part; and additionally petitioner claims actual and punitive damages in the sum of **$10,000,000.00 (ten million dollars)**, together with such other and further relief as may be just herein.*

Dated : Bronx, NY May 31, 1994

EGIDIO SEMENTILLI, pro se
2041 Colonial Avenue
Bronx, NY 10461
718-597-4642

EGIDIO SEMENTILLI, being duly sworn: I am the Petitioner in the within Article 78 proceeding; I have reading the foregoing petition and know the contents thereof; and the same is true to my own knowledge except to the matters therein stated to be alleged on information and belief and as to those matters I believe it to be true.

EGIDIO SEMENTILLI
Police Officer Exam No. 0294
List No. 6168

TO: NEW YORK CITY CIVIL SERVICE COMMISSION
ONE CENTRE STREET
NEW YORK, NY 10007

1. I, Egidio Sementilli respond to the determination Dated April 7,1994 by challenging the validity of the disqualifying psychological and/or psychiatric rhetoric, referred to herein, falsely and prejudicially as "evidence" being a word used to misrepresent or as a substitute for "opinion" or the state of someone else's mind. This is an unconstitutional substitute for due process of law. See US v. Reynolds, 98 US 145 (1878).

2. I further submit that the very words "psychological" or "psychiatric" are offensive to me on religious grounds, as a devoted adherent of the Roman Catholic religious faith. This is so because the purported "procedures" are efforts to examine my soul. By definition "psychology" is the study of the "soul" an abstract essence of the human condition of metaphysical dimensions, simply stated beyond objective definition. Academic charlatans have fraudulently applied "psychology" behind the cachet of medicine to the human "mind" without supplying any objective data measurable in any cognizable form. Academic charlatans engage in the use of concepts, bedimmed in purported mathematical formulas foisted as "statistics" to enslave the human victims in their reach; and psychiatry is by definition involved with the cure of the "soul". For these efforts the First Amendment guarantees me the right to go to my priest and bishop. Hence these efforts are in violation of US v. Reynolds supra as well and other Constitutional protection.

3. I further submit that recourse to the challenged efforts, in addition to their religious nature, are intended as a scheme of enslavement by conscripting the mind and the body into compliance with efforts to exploit the human condition and circumvent the right to exercise Constitutionally guaranteed civil and human rights under color of law with fraudulently conceived standards of performance which reflect a "hatred" protocol of ethno-racial and religious bias raising the examining tyrant's "opinion" to a level of expert knowledge not scientifically demonstrable. This is especially so when inked besmirched paper is referred to as a "Rohrscach" test and other fabrication couched in the religion of statistics.

4. The purported "battery of psychological tests consisting of the Minnesota Multi-Phasic Personality Inventory, the Cornell Index and the California Psychological Inventory, and the House-Tree Projective Test, in addition I completed a Police Candidate Questionnaire". These purported "tests" are arbitrary, capricious, unreasonable and are contrived to support protected corruption and the financial interests of the so called "testing" industry and their collaborators for political objectives established by the Department as a "pecking order" of illegal discrimination that can only be available through expensive litigation to invoke rulings of the US Supreme Court and/or Article 78 petitions to deny unfairly, access to employment of traditionally discriminated minorities of the Afro-American, Roman Catholic or Hispanic communities. The same statistical suggestions used by the examining tyrants may be used to demonstrate the stated illegal forms of minority discrimination in the testing procedure.

5. I have been denied access to information and discovery and inspection of data supporting the purported validity of the procedures of "disqualification" perfidiously masked as "confidential". This illegal denial of access is purportedly justified by Matter of Tamalo v. Murphy 38 NY 2d 637, but falsely and in violation of Al Khaz Raji v. St Francis College, 481 US 604 and Shaare Tefila v. Cobb 481. US 615. These Supreme Court decisions hold that delegated quasi judicial/legislative authority my not be applied without a hearing in any case in which the respondent is a member of a traditionally recognized minority sounding in racial, cultural, ethnic, and / or gender discrimination in support of purported denial of enforcement of Constitutionally protected rights.

6. The so called testing effort is in commercial conflict with the interest of authority of the Police Department, because it burdens the public effort with financial exploitation by organized Lawyers, psychologists, psychiatrists, judges and other socially unproductive institutions in symbiosis with parasitic waste to perpetuate traditional minority religious and economic district in as a substitute for the rule of law outlawing said conduct by the examining tyrants in public or private efforts, in a manner of punishment for heresy without crime reminiscent of the terrors of the Roman Inquisition led by Tomas Torquemada who performed his cruelty without mercy.

7. I submit that the Commission is acting in bad faith, because it provided me with the Matter of Murphy v. Tamalo supra with further material guaranteeing only the financial enrichment of the Commission's partners in crime in the so called testing procedure. Simply stated: Whatever opinion I might furnish from so called "experts" I lose because of Murphy v. Tamalo. I, of course follow the ruling of the US Supreme Court in US v. Reynolds, 98 US 148 which established the rule: " The civil magistrate may not intrude into the field of opinion" which rule is taken from the language of the Virginia Statute Religious Freedoms prohibiting government intrusion into areas where no objective validity can be established which, as we see describes psychiatry though not for example neurology wherein a dispute as to the presence of a brain tumor can be resolved by the objective evidence of an X-Ray picture.

8. Psychology and psychiatry are inherently anti-semitic and anti-Roman Catholic because both ideologies reject the scriptural premise for the Messianic redemption of the Jewish existence and denies Roman Catholics forgiveness sins, classifying any adherence to a metaphysical concept as a mental disorder akin to insanity.

9. The bad faith of the examining tyrants is further evidenced by a complete refusal to assist me in determining where and how the purported finding of disqualification was related to my mind or my soul. The examining tyrants, could honestly evaluate my qualifications for work by asking me to perform a reasonably work related task. It is unlikely that a police officer will ever be required to read an ink blot (Rohrschack test) for interpretive reasons in his regular employment or psychological inventory test or other religious test.

10. For the sake of clarity, the religion in question is the belief that behavior does not derive from free will and can be predicted by the opinion of a biased ethno-religious bigot and such "religion" is not available by digging into the ground or be manufactured in a laboratory, and has only rhetorical existence in fraudulently compiled statistics.

11. DSM 3r is the deceptive name for Diagnostic and Statistical Manual, third edition revised, a bible used to classify all of humanity as suffering from a mental disorder in the words of the Wall Street Journal of April 14, 1993 to support fraudulent aspects of the "health industry". Hence the "statistical" theses must be totally disregarded as a standard of performance in police employment because they are derived from laboratory observations of lower forms of life, deliberately to apply non-intellectual paradigms of conduct from life forms that are unable to exercise the intellectual privilege, in its dehumanization effort upon those human victims targeted for manipulation, enslavement and exploitation to systems of protected corruption of economic and ideological oppression, rather than honest public service. This fraudulent effort fails in compliance with Constitutional standards, especially Sixth Amendment guarantee of confrontation of accusing witnesses and cross examination under oath.

12. My Roman Catholic soul is also available for examination by an appropriate Roman Catholic priest and I will give him my confession following traditional ritual usage under the condition that such examination by a Roman Catholic priest be institutionalized as compliance and qualification for the position that I seek. I offer this effort as responsive to your psychological criterion purporting to examine my mind.

13. Civil Service Commission rule 2-02(g) is vague and inappropriate in failing to objectively define medical documentation resulting from institutionalized fraudulent academic submissions in the metaphor of cult ritual frequently referred to as "devil worship" in medieval times. Your metaphor of "devil worship" relates to the "interpretation" of "stigmata diaboli" (devil marks) such as scars, moles, freckles, strabismus, club foot, winespots etc., substituted by your fraudulent and racketeering academic with two dimensional marks on paper.

14. I have always been available for scientific medical evaluation of blood, urine, tissue, bones cartilage, mucous, skin, and I will submit my mind for such examination as can be objectively distinguished from my Roman Catholic soul.

15. Devil worship camouflages artful rhetoric in the context of "secular humanism" as a substitute for ethno-religious discrimination otherwise outlawed in violation of my civil rights and racketeering in violation of 18 USC 1961 et seq. (RICO) and illegal restraint of trade by snuffing out marketplace competition for the position I seek as a life time career.

16. New York City Civil Service Commission is a bureaucratic fraud to institutionalize discrimination to apply hatred protocols by the police department to perpetuate customary prejudice with pseudo-medical religious hatred in a fraudulent statutory rubric.

17. Psychological "performance test" was institutionalized by the Police department to attempt to legally discriminate against non image conforming minorities threatened in consequence of broad civil rights legislation of the 1960's in federal and state contexts.

18. New York Civil Service Commission is a redundant fraudulent "damage control" effort to usurp and conceal entrenched police department protected discrimination and inherent corruption in consequence thereof. Remedial policies to increase minority representation in the police department are systematically defeated and circumvented by the pseudo-medical, religious and ritualistic "psychological test" screening procedures honed to perpetuate entrenched discriminatory patterns of personnel recruitment.

19. The Department of Personnel is the oversight agency of the Civil Service Commission and for personnel recruitment of all public employment and is the responsible agency for the discrimination delegated to the Civil Service Commission, and must be enjoined and sanction for such illegal recruitment procedures. The Civil Service Commission is redundant and must be dissolved of all pretenses of recruitment authority.

[illegible] Dow, a recent United States Supreme Court ruling expertise cannot be supported as valid when based solely on a general consensus of the adherents of the alleged field of expertise, but must be supported by objectively quantifiable substanive criteria. The purported "psychological disqulaification" do not meet this standard and are invalid except as a racketeering and fraudulent effort upon the City of New York and its employees.

For all of the above reasons, I request the New York City Civil Service Commission and or the Department of Personnel to vacate the finding of "disqualified for psychological reasons" and facilitate the approval of my employment application and payment of seniority and wages and promotional considerations due me retroactively to the time of my first application and qualification.

Sworn to and subscribed
before me this 31 day of May 1994

EGIDIO JOSEPH SEMENTILLI
2041 Colonial Avenue
Bronx, NY 10461
Police Officer Exam No. 0294
List No. 6168

Notary public
Gene Crescenzi
5856050 Bronx County,New York
Commission Expires September 30,1994
this 31 day of May 1994

LEGAL AUTHORITIES AND ARGUMENTS

PREAMBLE TO DECLARATION OF INDEPENDENCE

We hold these truths to be self evident, that all men are created equal, that they are endowed with certain unalienable rights, that among these are life, liberty and the pursuit of happiness.

TABLE OF CASES RELIED ON

Daubert v. Dow,Docket # 92-102

Stewart v. Pearce, 484 F. 2d 1031 (9th Cir. 1973)

Strauss v. Hannig, 169 Misc. 29 NY 2d 102, affd 281 NY 612, 22 N.E. 2d 174

Horowitz v. Anker, 437 F. Supp. 495, (1977, affd 578 F. 2d 1368)

Lombard v. Bd of Education, 502 F. 2d 631, (2d Cir. 1974) cert. denied 420 US 976 (1975)

Newman v. Bd of Education, 508 F. 2d 277 (1979) Cert denied 420 U.S. 104 (1975) remanded

Reynolds v. U.S. 98 US 145 (1878)

In re Grand Jury 91-5047 and 91-5049 (2d Circuit)

Lamont v. Woods, 948 F. 2d 825 (1991)

Bd of Education v. Barnett. 319 US 624 (1943)

Torcaso v. Watkins, 367 US 488 (1961), pg. 495

Brisco v. Lahue, 460 US 325, 103 S.Ct 1108, 75 L. E D 2d 98 (1983)

Al Khaz Raji v. St. Francis College, 481 US 604 (1987)

sementilli

Shaare Tefila v. Cobb, 481 US 615 (1987)

Nassau Neuropsychiatric Society v. Adelphi University, 275 NYS 2d 511

STATUTES

42 USC 1981 to 1985

18 USC 1961 et seq. (RICO)

UNITED STATES CONSTITUTION

ARTICLE VI

FIRST AMENDMENT

FIFTH AMENDMENT

SIXTH AMENDMENT

THIRTEENTH AMENDMENT

FOURTEENTH AMENDMENT

SUPERIOR AUTHORITY

IN GOD WE TRUST

sementilli

APEX
TP
9780160461149
76901945 – 15